MICHAEL DAVITT

Historical Association of Ireland
Life and Times Series, No. 14

Michael Davitt

CARLA KING

Published for the
HISTORICAL ASSOCATION OF IRELAND
By Dundalgan Press Ltd

First published 1999
ISBN 0-85221-138-4

For Jonah

Cover design: Jarlath Hayes
Cover illustration: Michael Davitt, studio portrait. Davitt Papers,
TCD, MS 9649/16. The permission of the
Board of Trinity College Dublin, for reproduction
of the photograph is gratefully acknowledged.
Historical Association of Ireland, Dublin
Printed by Dundalgan Press, Dundalk

FOREWORD

This series of short biographical studies published by the Historical Association of Ireland is designed to place the lives of leading historical figures against the background of new research on the problems and conditions of their times. These studies should be particularly helpful to students preparing for Leaving Certificate, G.C.E. Advanced Level and undergraduate history examinations, while also appealing to the general public.

CIARAN BRADY
Historical Association of Ireland

PREFACE

I would like to thank Ciaran Brady for inviting me to write this book and for coping stoically with delays and computer breakdowns on my part. I am also very grateful to Colm Croker for his meticulous and expert copy-editing.

I am deeply indebted to Alan O'Day, Pauric Travers and my father, Justin Keating, for reading and commenting on draft versions. I take full responsibility for any errors that remain.

I should like to pay tribute to the support and encouragement of my colleagues Pauric Travers, Jimmy Kelly, Dáire Keogh and Patrick O'Donoghue in the History Department, St Patrick's College, Drumcondra.

I thank the Board of Trinity College, Dublin, for permission to quote from the Davitt Papers. In the case of two references in the Davitt Papers it proved impossible to identify copyright-holders, and I offer my apologies to them. I also gratefully acknowledge the assistance of librarians and archivists in Trinity College, St Patrick's College, the National Library of Ireland and University College Dublin.

Finally my thanks to my son Jonah, who patiently endured maternal neglect and preoccupation while this was being written.

CARLA KING
History Department
St Patrick's College, Drumcondra

CONTENTS

CHRONOLOGY OF DAVITT'S LIFE AND TIMES

1846 25 Mar.: Michael Davitt born in Straide, County Mayo, to Catherine (*née* Kielty) and Martin Davitt, small tenant farmers.

1850 Sept.(?): Davitt family evicted; they emigrate to Haslingden, Lancashire.

1857 8 May: Davitt in accident at Stellfoxe's Victoria Mill, following which his right arm is amputated. He is sent to John Poskett's school, Haslingden.

1861 Aug.(?): begins work in Haslingden post office, run by Henry Cockcroft.

1865 Joins the Irish Republican Brotherhood; shortly after elected 'centre' of the Rossendale 'circle' of the I.R.B.

1867 11 Feb.: leads a detachment of Fenians from Haslingden to take part in the abortive raid on Chester Castle, he and his men retreating undetected on realising that the police have been informed of it in advance. 5–6 Mar.: unsuccessful Fenian rising in Ireland.

1868 Appointed organising secretary and arms agent of the I.R.B. for England and Scotland.

1869 July: resigns from his employment in Haslingden to become full-time Fenian activist.

1870 14 May: arrested and charged with treason-felony. 18 July: sentenced to 15 years' penal servitude. 1 Aug.: Landlord and Tenant (Ireland) Act, 1870 (33 & 34 Vict., c. 46) passed. 29 June: Amnesty Association founded, with Isaac Butt as president. 28 Sept.: Butt founds Home Government Association.

1871 Dec.: death of Martin Davitt at Scranton, Pennsylvania.

1872 18 July: Ballot Act introduces secret voting.

1875 19 Apr.: Parnell enters House of Commons.

1877 31 July–1 Aug.: Parnell and Biggar undertake obstruction of House of Commons business. 19 Dec.: Davitt released on ticket-of-leave.

1878 13 Jan.: Davitt and three other released Fenians arrive in Dublin. 26 Jan.: Davitt travels on to Connacht. 4 Feb.: returns to England to campaign for release of remaining

1

Fenian prisoners. 9 Mar.: first address to large public meeting at St James's Hall, London. 12 May: Davitt tries unsuccessfully to persuade Parnell to join I.R.B. 20 June: gives oral evidence to the Kimberley Commission on Penal Reform (having already submitted written evidence). July–Dec.: on lecture tour in U.S., where he visits his family and meets John Devoy and other leaders of Irish-American nationalism. 24 Oct.: Devoy sends telegram to James O'Connor offering conditional support of Irish-American Fenians to Parnell. 27 Dec.: Devoy's 'New Departure' letter published in *Freeman's Journal.*

1879   19–26 Jan.: attends meeting in Paris in unsuccessful attempt to win I.R.B. leadership support for 'New Departure'. 6 Apr.: first meeting of Davitt and Devoy with Parnell in Dublin to try to win his support for 'New Departure'. 20 Apr.: Irishtown meeting, County Mayo. 8 (?) May: Davitt removed from Supreme Council of I.R.B. 1 June: second meeting of Davitt and Devoy with Parnell, Dublin. 8 June: Westport meeting, addressed by Davitt and Parnell. 16 Aug.: National Land League of Mayo founded, Castlebar. 21 Oct.: Irish National Land League founded, Imperial Hotel, Dublin; Davitt elected secretary. 19 Nov.: arrest of Davitt, James Daly and James Bryce Killen on charge of sedition; held in Sligo jail; released on bail, 25 Nov.

1880   11 Mar.: Parnell launches Irish Land and Industrial League of the United States. 9 May: Davitt leaves for U.S. to join Dillon in campaign for funds and to organise Irish National Land League of the United States. 18 May: on Davitt's arrival in New York, national convention of Irish National Land League of the United States elects him secretary, in which post he agrees to serve for the duration of his visit. 18 July: death of Catherine Davitt at Manayunk, Pennsylvania. 18 Sept.: Davitt first meets Mary Yore, Oakland, California, whom he is later to marry. 15 Oct.: Ladies' Land League established, New York. 20 Nov.: returns from the U.S. Dec.: First Anglo-Boer War breaks out.

1881   24 Jan.: Protection of Person and Property Bill introduced in House of Commons (enacted 2 Mar.). 27–28 Jan.: meeting in House of Commons and later Westminster Palace Hotel considers but rejects plan to withdraw Irish Party from House of Commons, set up a national convention in Dublin and launch a 'no rent' campaign. 31 Jan.: Irish Ladies' Land League launched under the leadership of Anna Parnell. 3 Feb.: Davitt's ticket-of-leave is revoked and he is imprisoned once again, in Portland prison in Dorset. 7 Apr.: Land Law (Ireland) Bill introduced in House of Commons (enacted 22 Aug.). 13 Oct.: arrest of Parnell (arrests of other leaders follow) and imprisonment in Kilmainham jail without trial, under provisions of the Protection of Person and Property Act. 18 Oct.: 'No Rent Manifesto' launched. 20 Oct.: Land Court opens; Land League proclaimed an unlawful organisation. Dec.: Ladies' Land League proclaimed an unlawful organisation.

1882   2 May: Parnell, Dillon and J. J. O'Kelly released under the terms of the 'Kilmainham Treaty'. 6 May: Davitt released; that evening Lord Frederick Cavendish, Chief Secretary, and T. H. Burke, Under-Secretary, assassinated in Phoenix Park. 15 May: Arrears Bill introduced in House of Commons. 6 June: Davitt makes first speech advocating land nationalisation. 3 Aug.: in meeting with Parnell, Davitt proposes the establishment of a new movement, 'The National Land and Industrial Union of Ireland'. 8 Aug.: Ladies' Land League dissolved. 18 Aug.: Arrears of Rent (Ireland) Act, 1882 (45 & 46 Vict., c. 47) passed. 13 Sept.: 'Avondale Treaty' with Parnell. 17 Oct.: Irish National League founded, Dublin.

1883   8 Feb.–4 June: Davitt and T. M. Healy serve four months in prison for sedition. 11 Dec.: Parnell receives cheque for over £37,000 as testimonial at public meeting, Rotunda, Dublin.

1884   1 Nov.: Gaelic Athletic Association founded, Thurles. 6 Dec.: Representation of the People Act passed (Irish electorate increased from 126,000 to 738,000). Dec.: *Leaves from a Prison Diary* published (dated 1885).

1885   Jan.: Davitt visits France and Italy; interview with Kossuth in Turin. 24 Jan.: dynamite explosions in Westminster Hall, House of Commons and the Tower of London. Apr.: Davitt visits Palestine and Egypt. May: travelling in Switzerland and Germany. 14 Aug.: Purchase of Land (Ireland) Act, 1885 (48 & 49 Vict., c. 73) ('Ashbourne Act') passed. 21 Nov.: Parnell issues manifesto calling on Irish in Great Britain to vote against Liberal Party in coming elections. 17 Dec.: Herbert Gladstone flies 'Hawarden kite', indicating that W. E. Gladstone favours Home Rule. Davitt invited to stand as workingmen's candidate for Sheffield; declines.

1886   27 Jan.: Conservative government resigns. 1 Feb.: Gladstone becomes Prime Minister for third time. 8 Apr.: First Home Rule Bill introduced in House of Commons. 9 June: defeat of First Home Rule Bill. 1–17 July: general election; Conservative victory. 23 Oct.: Plan of Campaign launched. c. 9–10 Dec.: meeting between Parnell and William O'Brien to discuss Plan of Campaign. 18 Dec.: Plan of Campaign proclaimed 'an unlawful and criminal conspiracy'. 30 Dec.: Davitt marries Mary Yore at Oakland, California.

1887   Davitt presented with Land League cottage, Ballybrack. Mar.–Dec.: London *Times* publishes series of articles on 'Parnellism and Crime'. June: Bodyke evictions, County Clare.

1888   20 Apr.: papal rescript condemns Plan of Campaign. 13 Aug.: Special Commission on 'Parnellism and Crime' established.

1889   24–31 Oct.: evidence for defence before Special Commission. 25 Oct.: Tenants' Defence Association formed; Davitt becomes a member of its council. Nov.: Liverpool dock strike, in which Davitt serves as mediator.

1890   Davitt living in London. 21 Jan.: Irish Democratic Trade and Labour Federation founded in Cork, with Davitt as president. 13 Feb.: report of Special Commission on Parnellism and Crime. Mar.: acts as arbitrator in dispute between Dublin United Builders' Labourers' Union and employers. 25 Apr.–3 May: strike of workers on Great Southern and Western Railway in which Davitt and Archbishop Walsh act as mediators. 1 Sept.: *Labour World* launched, London, with Davitt as editor (ceases publication, May 1891). 17 Nov.: Captain O'Shea granted decree *nisi* in divorce proceedings. 22 Nov.: Davitt in editorial in *Labour World* calls for Parnell's temporary retirement as leader of the Irish Parliamentary Party. 6 Dec.: Irish Parliamentary Party splits over Parnell divorce case. 8–22 Dec.: Davitt organises anti-Parnellite campaign in North Kilkenny by-election. Publication of *The 'Times'–Parnell Commission: Speech delivered by Michael Davitt in Defence of the Land League.*

1891   3–11 Feb.: Boulogne negotiations between Parnell, O'Brien and Dillon. 10 Mar.: anti-Parnellite section leaves the National League and establishes the National Federation, of which Davitt becomes secretary. 2 Apr.: North Sligo by-election, in which Davitt acts as organiser, won by anti-Parnellite candidate. Davitt travels to U.S. (returns early 1892). 5 Aug.: Purchase of Land (Ireland) Act, 1891 (54 & 55 Vict., c. 48) passed. 6 Oct.: death of Parnell. 23 Dec.: Waterford City by-election; Davitt defeated by John Redmond.

1892   July: Davitt elected M.P. for North Meath but result overturned on petition; declared bankrupt as a consequence. 14 Aug.: acts as arbitrator in conflict between Polish and Russian revolutionaries in London.

1893   19 Jan.: Gladstone introduces Second Home Rule Bill in House of Commons. 8 Feb.: Davitt elected M.P. for North-East Cork. 11 Apr.: maiden speech in House of Commons in support of Home Rule Bill. 9 Sept.: Home Rule Bill defeated in House of Lords.

1894   27 Apr.: Irish Trade Union Congress founded. 15 Aug.: Irish Land and Labour Association founded.

1895   Apr.: Kathleen Davitt, eldest daughter, dies, aged seven. Apr.–Nov: Davitt on lecture tour in Australia and New Zealand. 20 July: general election; Davitt elected M.P. for South Mayo. 7 Nov.: executive of Irish National League of Great Britain expels Healy and replaces him with Davitt.

1896 2 Feb.: resignation of Justin McCarthy as leader of anti-Parnellites; replaced by John Dillon. Apr.: Davitt's family joins him in London; they rent a house in Battersea. 1–3 Sept.: Irish Race Convention at Leinster Hall, Dublin.

1897 Apr.–June: Davitt in U.S. lobbying senators against the proposed Anglo-American Arbitration Treaty.

1898 Celebration of centenary of 1798 rising, in which Davitt takes part. 23 Jan.: United Irish League founded by William O'Brien. Jan: publication of *Life and Progress in Australasia*. 12 Aug.: Local Government (Ireland) Act, 1898 (61 & 62 Vict., c. 37).

1899 Mar.(?): Davitt and family move back to Ireland; reside in Mount Salus, Dalkey. 11 Oct.: Second Anglo-Boer War breaks out. 25 Oct.: Davitt resigns from House of Commons in protest against Boer War.

1900 30 Jan.: reunification of Irish Parliamentary Party. 26 Mar.: Davitt arrives in Pretoria, having travelled to South Africa as war correspondent; returns to Ireland in July.

1902 May: publication of *The Boer Fight for Freedom*. 3 Sept.: publication of Captain John Shawe-Taylor's letter. Sept.: Davitt travels to U.S. (returns early 1903). Oct.: publication of Davitt's pamphlet *Some Suggestions for a Final Settlement of the Land Question*.

1903 3 Jan.: report of Dunraven Land Conference. 25 Mar.: Chief Secretary George Wyndham introduces land bill based on recommendations of Land Conference. 19 Apr.: Kishinev pogrom. 22–31 May: Davitt in Russia to investigate pogrom for *New York American Journal*. 14 Aug.: Irish Land Act, 1903 (3 Edw. VII, c. 37) (Wyndham Land Act) passed. Dec.: publication of *Within the Pale: The True Story of Anti-Semitic Persecutions in Russia*.

1904 Jan.: Davitt denounces antisemitic sermon of Redemptorist priest, Father John Creagh, in Limerick. Feb.–Apr.: Davitt family in U.S. May: publication of *The Fall of Feudalism in Ireland*. June: visits Russia for *New York American Journal*, where he meets Tolstoy. Defends Dublin and District Tramwaymen's Union in its claims against the Dublin Tramway Company.

1905 Jan.–Feb.: Davitt in Russia investigating 'Bloody Sunday' and unrest that followed in St Petersburg, Moscow, Helsinki and Warsaw. Labour Representation Committee formed.

1906 Jan.: campaigns in British general election on behalf of Labour Party. 15 Jan.: letter in *Freeman's Journal* by Bishop of Limerick, Edward O'Dwyer, urges Irish support for Conservative Party on denominational education. 22 Jan.: Davitt in letter to *Freeman's Journal* defends state-aided, secular education. 16 Feb.: takes part in victory celebrations in Queen's Hall, London, for 29 seats won by Labour Party. 30 May: dies in Elpis Nursing Home, Lower Mount Street, Dublin; buried in Straide, County Mayo.

INTRODUCTION

Since his lifetime Michael Davitt has remained something of a national icon, revered as the father of the Land League, which won for Irish tenant farmers the right to own their own land. Yet, as Paul Bew has pointed out, while 'few openly disputed Davitt's ideals . . . many quietly and privately disavowed them'.[1] For Davitt was a radical, struggling against a growing conservatism that sought to contain what he had no hesitation in calling an agrarian revolution. What he sought for Ireland was a far more egalitarian solution to the land question than that which eventuated.

Davitt remains an important figure, partly because his input was formative at a critical point in Irish history, at the beginning of the defeat of landlordism by the rising middle-class Catholic tenants. It was largely as a result of the marshalling of Irish public opinion around the Land League/Irish Parliamentary Party coalition, which Davitt played a crucial part in achieving, and in which popular grievances and nationalist sentiment were combined in a new and powerful mixture, that Home Rule became a realistic proposition in the 1880s. At the same time, the closing decades of the nineteenth century marked the point at which Irish society turned, at which, in Samuel Clark's terms, the 'challenging collectivity' of the 'comfortable' middle-class Catholic farmers and rural bourgeoisie overcame the 'retreating collectivity' of Irish landlords.[2] It was a vitally important development for the trajectory of Irish society.

In his political development, Davitt made the transition between two political traditions in Ireland, the physical-force approach of the Fenians and the constitutional one of the Irish Parliamentary Party. To this he added the radicalism of the industrial England in which he had been raised and with which his contacts remained strong throughout his life, and the bond with Irish-America, which was to play an influential role in Irish affairs from his time on. In a sense his career mirrors the interplay of forces that made up the 'Irish question' in the late nineteenth century.

Moreover, Davitt's concerns extended well beyond Ireland: he sympathised with national struggles in Poland, Finland, Hungary and other countries; he took the Boer side in the Anglo-Boer wars; and he was a passionate advocate of social reform everywhere, whether in the improvement of prison conditions, or the rights of Kanaka labour in Australia, or the conditions of Jews in Russia.

Largely self-taught but widely read, Davitt was perhaps the most original thinker among Irish nationalists of his day. His ideas show a clear evolution from the Fenianism of his early years to the internationalism and social radicalism of his later career, while his commitment to Irish nationalism never wavered. Yet the originality of his ideas set him, to some extent, outside the mainstream of Irish political life. He entered parliament only reluctantly in 1893 and was glad to leave it six years later; his main political achievements were outside Westminster. His work as a journalist and public speaker, by which he earned his living throughout his adult life, and his six books, all helped to shape popular opinion in Ireland, Britain, America and Australia in his day.

Davitt's warm personality, the hardships of his life and, above all, his identification with the downtrodden have made him a much-loved figure in Irish history, the equal, perhaps, of his contemporary, Charles Stewart Parnell. It is surprising, therefore, given the extent of attention paid to the more enigmatic Parnell, that with the important exception of Professor T. W. Moody's work (published in articles and in his definitive biography, *Davitt and Irish Revolution, 1846-82*)[3] and a handful of significant articles,[4] there has been comparatively so little recent research on Davitt's career and ideas.

A short biography such as this cannot hope to do full justice to Davitt's life and thought. The aim here is to introduce the reader to the range of his activities and interests and to situate them in the context of his time. What it is hoped will emerge is the extent to which he is a more complex and interesting figure than the traditional image of the son of an evicted tenant who later helped to smash landlordism—although that too is part of the story.

1

BACKGROUND AND EARLY YEARS, 1846–77

Among the best-known features of Michael Davitt's career, both during his lifetime and since, is the series of adversities he faced in his childhood and youth. Born on 25 March 1846, in Straide, County Mayo, the son of Catherine and Martin Davitt, small tenant farmers, one of his earliest memories was of his family's eviction from their home. Then aged four, he witnessed their house pulled down and underwent the experience of emigration to the Lancashire industrial town of Haslingden. He was to comment that all the family's ills stemmed from that eviction,[1] these formative memories lending a certain edge to his political outlook, in particular to his approach to the land question in Ireland. As he wrote later, 'The men who made the Land League were the sons of those who went through the horrors of the Great Famine',[2] among which eviction figured prominently.

Part of the 1,000-strong Irish community in Haslingden, Martin and Catherine Davitt found work in fruit-hawking and in various other casual occupations. The family shared a house with other immigrants, encountering the antagonism of British workers who viewed the impoverished Irish as a threat to wage levels.[3] Thrown together in a hostile environment, the Irish community developed strong bonds based on their social life, religion and language. The Davitt family, like most of the Irish community around them, were native Irish speakers, but Martin Davitt, who spoke English and could read and write, helped neighbours by writing their letters and ran a night school in the house. The home of their neighbour, Molly Madden, was a centre for music, dancing and storytelling.

Michael Davitt was nine years old when he left his primary school and started work in the cotton mills of Haslingden. Two years later, while tending a machine, his right arm was caught and crushed, necessitating its amputation ten days later. It was one of many such industrial accidents, for which no compensation was ever paid.

For the poor, such a disability was likely to mean marginalisation and dependence on relatives or on the most menial and insecure work. For Davitt and his family, the accident was certainly a tragedy. However, it was to save a bright child from what might have been a lifetime of mill work. When he had recovered his health he was sent, with the help of a philanthropic manufacturer, John Dean, to a local Wesleyan school and given a good education for a further four years. This provided him with a foundation on which he continued to build all his life, becoming a wide and avid reader. In the short term, it enabled him, in August 1861, to find work in Haslingden post office, run by Henry Cockcroft, who also had a small printing business. He was to retain happy memories of both school and Cockcroft's employment. Therefore, although Davitt and his family had experienced hostility and difficulty in England, he had also met with encouragement.

It is here that Davitt's development shares some of the formative features of a British working-class radical, and one might look for the source of some of his later attitudes to this period of his life.[4] He became a member of the Mechanics' Institute, where he continued to read and study at night. He attended lectures and came in touch with the Chartist leader Ernest Jones, whom he was later to describe as the first Englishman he ever heard denouncing landlordism in Ireland. While in political terms Chartism was by the 1860s a spent force, it had been strong in Lancashire and many of its ideas were still current there. Thus by his late teens Davitt might have followed the path of the upwardly mobile working-class radical. That he did not is attributable to his involvement with Fenianism.

Davitt joined the Fenians in 1865, at the age of nineteen. It was a natural step to take: many of the young men of the Irish immigrant community would have supported the movement. As Frank Haran, a contemporary and fellow-Fenian, related, it was said in Haslingden that 'every smart respectable young fellow' was a member.[5] Moreover, Davitt later commented that there was a certain family tradition of being 'agin the government',[6] and his father had been a member of a Ribbon society in the 1830s, Mayo being one of the strongest centres of Ribbonism in Ireland. Both

Martin and Catherine Davitt knew and approved of their son's membership of the Irish Republican Brotherhood, though they may not have been aware how high or how rapidly he rose within the movement. He was soon elected 'centre' of the Rossendale 'circle' of the I.R.B., a cell of about fifty members. He led a detachment of Fenians in the ill-conceived attack on Chester Castle in February 1867, withdrawing his men and enabling them to return to their homes undetected when it became clear that the plan had been made known to the authorities and the police were lying in wait for them.

In 1868, when he was twenty-two, Davitt was appointed organising secretary and arms agent of the I.R.B. for England and Scotland. This meant that he had to resign from Cockcroft's employment and spend the next two years in the guise of a hawker, moving from place to place, furtively meeting with other Fenians and organising arms shipments to Ireland. From February 1867, even before the unsuccessful Fenian rising in Ireland, there was a police file on Davitt in Dublin Castle, although he was effective in covering his tracks to the extent that his importance in the movement was not grasped until later.

From its inception the I.R.B. was infiltrated by police informers. Such individuals were considered traitors by the movement and, in theory at least, were liable to be executed. In December 1869, in Manchester, a more flamboyant and incautious colleague of Davitt's, Arthur Forrester, denounced as a police spy another young Fenian from Salford, named Burke. Davitt's initial response was that he had no proof, and Forrester was forced to give way. While Davitt was elsewhere, Forrester renewed his charge, informing him by letter that he now had overwhelming proof against Burke and calling for his execution, failing which he would take the matter into his own hands. Davitt, in an effort to stop him, but convinced that direct prohibition would not be effective, wrote as if he was in agreement with Forrester but urged him not to go ahead until he had obtained the approval of two members of the I.R.B. Supreme Council, with whom Davitt was in touch. Thus, fatefully for Davitt, his letter appeared to condone murder, while his actual intention was to prevent it.[7] The letter's discovery by the police had two effects. One was to draw much increased police surveillance of his activities, through which the extent of his arms-smuggling activity was uncovered. The other was that the contents of the letter were used to incriminate Davitt during his trial for treason-felony in 1870.

Following several months of intensive police investigation, Davitt and John Wilson, the gunsmith with whom he had been dealing, were arrested separately on 14 May 1870 on the platform of Paddington railway station in London. At the trial, held in the Old Bailey in July, both men were found guilty of arms trafficking for the purpose of supporting a Fenian rising in Ireland. Davitt was sentenced to penal servitude for fifteen years, while Wilson received a seven-year sentence. The timing of their case was unfortunate. In March 1869 the newly elected Liberal Prime Minister, W. E. Gladstone, had released forty-nine Fenian prisoners in response to Isaac Butt's Amnesty campaign. This meant, however, that any further amnesties were likely to be postponed.

Thus, at the age of twenty-four, Davitt began a term of imprisonment which was to last seven and a half years of a fifteen-year sentence. Following the trial, he was imprisoned in Millbank penitentiary, where he was kept in solitary confinement and employed in oakum picking. Ten months later, on 25 May 1871, he was transferred to Dartmoor Public Works Prison, where he served the bulk of his sentence. He was first put to stone-breaking and then, when after a week his one hand was too blistered to continue, he was attached to a gang engaged in hauling carts around the prison. When the stump of his amputated arm was injured by the harness, he was returned to stone-breaking. He was also employed at pounding putrefying bones to be used as fertiliser; worked as a mason's labourer; and operated a wringing machine in the prison wash-house. Living conditions were very severe, prisoners being housed in tiny, inadequately lit or ventilated corrugated-iron cells, so airless that it was often necessary for Davitt to kneel with his mouth to the narrow opening at the bottom of the door to allow him to breathe without difficulty. The food rations were inadequate and infested with cockroaches, prisoners being sometimes reduced to eating candles to quell their hunger. They were also subjected to strip-searching four times a day, and Davitt, as a Fenian prisoner, was watched more closely than the other prisoners and seems to have been the recipient of more than the usual bullying and harassment by the warders.[8]

Nevertheless, it was through a friendly warder that Davitt was able to receive and to smuggle out letters, including one describing the conditions under which he was held, which was published in several Irish and English newspapers.[9] The controversy it provoked helped to strengthen the case of those who continued to campaign for his release. Eventually their efforts were to bear fruit in Davitt's release on ticket-of-leave on 19 December 1877.

While his health had been damaged by his prison experiences, Davitt, who in view of all that he had suffered, might have been forgiven for seeking to avoid any danger of reimprisonment, did not hesitate to throw himself back into Fenian activities. The campaign for his release had given him a public profile that he had not had before his imprisonment, so that he emerged a more formidable enemy of the British government than ever.[10]

His incarceration also left Davitt with a lasting concern for the welfare of prisoners and a desire to work for prison reform. Practically all radical nationalist leaders served terms of imprisonment; it was an occupational hazard of militant Irish nationalism. However, Davitt was the only one among them who, rather than emphasise the distinction between political and ordinary prisoners, set himself to improve the conditions of all, asking searching questions about what prisons were for and how they might be organised to serve to reform criminality rather simply to punish it.

Davitt's early background combines influences from Irish peasant society and British industrial life, as well as his experience of involvement in the Fenian organisation and a long term of imprisonment. His formative experiences diverged significantly from those of most of his contemporaries in the nationalist movement and were to send him in a different direction in later life. Already as a young man, his main preoccupations were along lines that were to characterise his life and work, a combination of a passion for social justice and a deep commitment to Irish nationalism. He had shown dedication to that movement and some leadership skills. But when he emerged from prison at the age of thirty-one, the Fenian movement was lacking in direction, and he had yet to work out his own future.

2

THE NEW DEPARTURE AND THE LAND LEAGUE, 1878–82

When Davitt was released from prison on ticket-of-leave on 19 December 1877, he travelled directly to London, where he was welcomed by Isaac Butt and other members of the Political Prisoners Visiting Committee. During more than seven years' incarceration he had thought deeply about the direction of Irish nationalism. The idea that he 'left prison with the Land League in his head' was lent support by Davitt himself, for example in his speech before the Special Commission on Parnellism and Crime, where he stated:

> The Land League, which is here on its trial, was largely, though not entirely, the offspring of thoughts and resolutions which whiled away many a dreary and lonely hour in political captivity. It lightened the burden of penal servitude, and brought compensating solace to some extent for the loss of liberty, of home, and of friends, to think, and reason, and plan, how, when freedom should once again restore me to the rights and privileges of society, I should devote to the good of Ireland what strength of purpose or ability of service long years of patient study and yearning aspirations should equip me with in a just cause.[1]

On the other hand, while he evidently felt the need for a new approach, it is unlikely, given his isolation from political life, that he worked out any detailed strategy. There is no evidence from his speeches following his release that he was thinking along the lines of establishing a Land League. He does seem to have wished, however, to see the Fenians adopt a less isolationist and a more political approach and to make contact with the Home Rule Party. His openness to the possibility of working with the party may have been strengthened by an appreciation of what Butt, 'Amnesty' Nolan, Parnell and others had done for Fenian prisoners, including himself, in the Amnesty movement and in parliament.

The following months were to see a very rapid evolution of Davitt's thought as he moved back into nationalist circles, rejoining the I.R.B. and being elected to the Supreme Council as representative for the north of England. Early in January 1878 he and the other three Fenian prisoners who had been released with him,[2] travelled to Dublin to be accorded a tumultuous reception. Soon after his arrival Davitt was invited to Mayo as the guest of James Daly, editor of the *Connaught Telegraph*. This gave him an opportunity to return to his birthplace of Straide, which he had not seen since early childhood. It also put him in touch with men such as James Daly in Mayo and Matthew Harris in Galway, who were already at the centre of agitation on behalf of small farmers in the west and were to play a large part in the land struggle in the future.

Back in England in February, Davitt threw himself into the campaign for the release of the remaining Fenian prisoners. Since regaining his freedom, popular attention had forced him into public speaking and writing, and he discovered that he had a taste for them. Moreover, attendance at meetings around Britain, most of which were organised by Fenians, brought him up to date with current thinking among radical nationalists, some of whom shared his belief in the need for a more flexible policy on the part of the I.R.B. Davitt's own area, northern England, seems to have been in the forefront of the demand for change. However, there was still a good deal of resistance to any departure from Fenian orthodoxy, particularly among the leadership.

Davitt's First Visit to America

In July 1878, seven months after his release from Dartmoor, Davitt made his first journey to America to visit his mother and sisters, his father having died in 1871. He intended to raise some money there by lecturing, to enable him to bring his mother and his youngest sister, Sabina, home to Ireland. That he would have contact with Clan na Gael was inevitable. J. J. O'Kelly, a close associate in the I.R.B., was a friend of the Clan na Gael leader John Devoy. Dr William Carroll of Philadelphia had already met Davitt in Ireland in 1877 and suggested that Clan na Gael help him by organising a series of lectures which would pay the expenses of his visit.[3] Immediately on his arrival in New York, then, Davitt became involved in political activities, as Devoy and Clan na Gael welcomed him with open arms. On their urging, he soon agreed to a much longer lecture tour than he had initially planned, remaining in America until December, when he returned, alone, to Ireland.

Davitt's first and most lasting links outside Ireland and Britain were with the United States. Since 1870, just a month before his arrest, when he had persuaded his parents and sister to move to America, all his close relatives were there, and he was later to marry an Irish-American woman, Mary Yore.

In certain respects Irish-American nationalism differed from the home-grown product. The emigrant experience shaped the Irish abroad. The loneliness they often faced and the need to survive in an alien atmosphere brought them together in social clubs and communities. They were overwhelmingly urban workers, often poor, humiliated and seeking social acceptance and respectability. For many, nationalist organisations offered them an identity and a means of self-assertion. Davitt, whose upbringing in Haslingden gave him an insight into such feelings, was able to tap into them:

> You want to be honoured among the elements that constitute this nation . . . You want to be regarded with the respect due you: that you may thus be looked on, aid us in Ireland to remove the stain of degradation from your birth . . . and [you] will get the respect you deserve.[4]

Irish-American nationalists differed somewhat in their political outlook from their counterparts in Ireland. They had encountered the American liberal democratic traditions of Thomas Jefferson and Andrew Jackson and adapted them to their own needs. Moreover, American society in the closing decades of the nineteenth century was undergoing rapid change and development. It had seen massive industrialisation and urbanisation in the years following the Civil War. American labour was becoming organised and radicalised in movements such as Powderly's Knights of Labour, and a strand of Irish-American nationalism was involved in, and influenced by, these organisations.

Although never a great orator, Davitt was, nevertheless, impressive and effective on a platform, speaking with a deep, resonant voice, tall and lean, with large brown eyes and black hair and beard, his manner serious and sincere. His dedication, his conviction and his willingness to undertake a gruelling tour throughout the country helped to invigorate a movement discouraged by the military failures of the Fenians and demoralised by the effects of an economic depression in the 1870s that had hit the vulnerable immigrant workers (including the Irish) badly. His tour was the first such venture on the part of the Clan, and in private meetings with Fenians in the towns and cities he visited Davitt attempted to revive flagging morale. But he too gained a great deal from his sojourn in the United States, which constituted what T. W. Moody has termed 'an indispensable stage in his political evolution'.[5] The American branch of Fenianism was more open to new strategies than its counterparts in England and Ireland. Thus Davitt participated in meetings and discussions where the policy of the 'New Departure' was hammered out. These months in America helped to radicalise him further and to deepen the social aspect of his thinking.

The New Departure

Davitt later denied that the 'New Departure', in terms of a formal alliance between Fenianism and the Irish Parliamentary Party, ever took place.[6] In that strict interpretation, he was correct. But what he, Devoy and others did advocate, and what in fact eventuated despite the opposition of the I.R.B. leadership, was an informal co-operation between Fenians on the one hand and parliamentarians on the other, coupled with a greater readiness on the part of both to address issues raised by the landlord–tenant struggle.

T. W. Moody distinguished three 'new departures' in the late nineteenth century. The first he dated from 1873, when the Fenians gave their support to Isaac Butt's Home Rule movement. The second involved the offer of support by Devoy and his followers in 1878 to the radical wing of the Home Rule Party, led by Parnell. The third was a rapprochement between the parliamentarians and the radical nationalists, both the I.R.B. rank and file in Ireland and Clan na Gael in America, in support of the Land League.[7]

The terms of the second 'new departure' were worked out between Davitt and Devoy in what R. V. Comerford has termed 'a fascinating dialogue-by-speechwriting' in the autumn of 1878.[8] Devoy's famous telegram to Parnell offering an alliance was sent without Davitt's knowledge, and he later condemned it as 'a most imprudent proceeding . . . an illustration of Irish "conspiracy as she was made"'.[9] In the event, the telegram was never passed on to Parnell, and although its contents were published, he ignored them.

The next task was to induce the leadership of the I.R.B. to accept the plan—not to abandon their revolutionary aims but to agree to support the efforts of the radical wing of the Home Rule Party. Davitt travelled to Paris in January 1879 to attend a conference of at least eight, or perhaps all eleven members of the Supreme Council.[10] The discussions lasted four days, but, with the exception of Matthew Harris of Ballinasloe, the Supreme Council members were unanimous in their hostility to the proposal. They did, however, agree to sanction the participation of individual members of the I.R.B. in the open movement, provided that they did not enter parliament (this permission was withdrawn a year later). In the event, the proposed second 'new departure' was to be superseded by the third.

Founding the Land League

It is inaccurate to suggest that the Fenians were uninterested in Irish agrarian problems. They deplored the landlord–tenant system and sought to end it. There had been some mutual suspicion between a largely urban-based Fenian rank and file and tenant farmers,[11] but more important was the fact that the Fenians saw the land question as soluble only in the context of self-government. The Home Rule Party too, and notably the English Radicals, such as John Stuart Mill, John Bright, Joseph Chamberlain, Charles Dilke and others, were aware of the problems. However, there was not much consensus about how they should be overcome and what to put in place of landlordism. While it seems that Davitt had not read James Fintan Lalor's work until 1880,[12] Devoy had; and moreover, knowledge of Lalor's suggestion that the land question should be linked to the national issue would have been current among Fenians. In a milieu that was preoccupied with Irish issues, it is highly likely that Davitt would have encountered Lalor's ideas.[13]

The economic crisis facing Irish tenant farmers in 1878–9 was, then, the catalyst needed to bring the sides together, but it was always to be a problematic alliance. A series of wet summers led to crop failures and consequent shortage. This was exacerbated by the onset of economic depression in Britain and the long-term effects of the transport revolution, which meant that large quantities of agricultural produce flooding onto the international market resulted in lower prices paid to farmers. The crisis was particularly marked in the west of Ireland, where small farmers, many of whom had depended on supplementing their income through migratory labour in Scotland and northern England, saw this support to their livelihood decline or disappear. Large numbers of them were deeply in debt to landlords and shopkeepers, and there was some fear of a recurrence of famine. Eviction levels were rising, but there was an increasing determination to resist.[14]

By the time Davitt returned from America in December 1878 concern was being voiced about the situation and about the need for an organisation to protect tenants against high rents and evictions. In February of the new year he visited the west of Ireland, where he was able to observe rising levels of distress for himself. It was this experience, coming as it did only weeks after the failure of the New Departure discussions in Paris, that seems to have led him toward a growing commitment to the land issue. At the time of his visit Daly and a group of men in the recently formed Mayo Tenants' Defence Association were already preparing a protest meeting against high rent levels to be held at Irishtown in April. Davitt joined them, and it was agreed that he would engage visiting speakers and draft resolutions for the meeting. Thus, from the beginning he was involved in shaping the course of the land movement, although he did not in fact attend the Irishtown meeting.

The Irishtown meeting on Sunday 20 April 1879 marked a new initiative in the countryside. It was large, the audience variously estimated from 4,000 to 13,000; it was peaceful; and it marked a coming together of farmers and townspeople, politicians and local leaders; moreover, it was not organised by the clergy. Though largely ignored by the press, it had an effect that tenants would appreciate: some landlords in Mayo and Galway responded promptly by allowing reductions and abatements in rent.

Following the success of the Irishtown meeting and despite clerical opposition, a further, larger protest was held at Westport on Sunday 8 June, attended and addressed by both Davitt and Parnell. This was the first time that the two men appeared on the same platform. Parnell had not yet committed himself fully to the land movement, though he had taken part in discussions with Davitt and Devoy, both anxious that he should lead the new movement. Nevertheless, a nucleus of suporters was forming, which included John Dillon, Andrew J. Kettle, leader of the Central Tenants' Defence Association, an organisation which had been campaigning on behalf of tenant farmers since the early 1870s, and Patrick Duggan, Bishop of Clonfert.

A series of mass meetings and demonstrations followed throughout the summer of 1879. On 16 August the National Land League of Mayo was established, on the basis of a programme and set of rules drawn up and proposed by Davitt. It was to provide the foundation for the national body, the Irish National Land League, launched two months later, on 21 October. At this point, with the formation of the National Land League, Parnell at last aligned himself unequivocally to the land movement, becoming its president and bringing about what T. W. Moody has termed the third new departure.[15] From the beginning, Fenians were at the core of the seven-man executive. Davitt, Thomas Brennan, both secretaries, Patrick Egan, the treasurer, and Joseph Gillis Biggar were all neo-Fenians, while William Henry O'Sullivan, another treasurer, was close to Fenianism. The two remaining members were Parnell and Andrew Kettle, the latter a moderate Home Ruler and the only farmer on the executive.

Davitt and Parnell

Over the period of almost two years since Davitt had been released from prison, he and Parnell had been in frequent contact and had developed considerable mutual respect. Born in the same year, though in very different circumstances, the two men have often been compared. Assessing the characters of the two, Davitt's biographer, T. W. Moody, pointed to some similarities:

> Behind very different exteriors they were both rather shy and lonely men, and with very different temperaments they both had proud and passionate natures.[16]

John Devoy described Parnell as in intellectual capacity unquestionably inferior to Davitt, whose better knowledge of the Irish people and training in Fenianism gave him an advantage. However, Davitt, in his view,

> was by nature an agitator and a preacher of ideas, rather than a politician, and his warm, impetuous temperament and impatience of difference of opinion unfitted him for the difficult role which leaders play in modern popular movements.[17]

Davitt appreciated what Parnell was trying to achieve at Westminster and understood some of the difficulties with which he had to grapple, while Parnell admired Davitt's courage and attributed to him much of the success of the land movement. With uncharacteristic enthusiasm, he was to express his approval of Davitt in Montreal in 1880, describing him as a man of humble origins who had 'raised himself and benefited by the opportunities given him for education in a most wonderful manner', continuing: 'Would that I could find words to express to you what I feel towards the man who has done so much in raising his country from degradation.'[18] Although they were never close friends, the sympathy between the two men was to persist, despite many tests upon it, up to the divorce crisis of 1890.

Land League Aims

Before the foundation of the Land League tenants' demands had been primarily about the conditions of their tenure, in particular for lower rents and more security of tenure. Even the radical priest of Partry, Father Patrick Lavelle, did not challenge the tenure system itself.[19] However, the Land League spokesmen, while presenting their aims as defensive, that is, protection of the tenant farmers of Ireland against rack-renting and eviction by landlords (the famous 'three Fs' of earlier reformers), in fact went much further. From the beginning the more radical of these made it clear that while striving to bring about a lowering of rents in the short term, the ultimate goal was the conversion of tenants into owner-occupiers. As Davitt stated at Claremorris on 13 July 1879:

> 'Fixity of tenure at fair rents' would do no longer. They must tell the English Legislature that the concession they gave would be taken as instalments only of their just demands, and they must not be satisfied with their representatives unless they supported the full demand, that the soil of Ireland should be returned to the people of Ireland.[20]

In the context of the time, the demand for peasant proprietorship was in itself quite radical. Despite the advocacy of reformers such as John Stuart Mill, it was not generally believed that a Westminster government, largely made up of landed proprietors, was ever likely to grant peasant proprietorship. For Davitt and some of his neo-Fenian associates such as Thomas Brennan and Patrick Egan, peasant proprietorship was not viewed as an end in itself, but as a lever in the struggle for Irish self-government. As they conceived it, once the demand for an abolition of landlordism was put and rejected, then Irish M.P.s would be justified in seceding from the Westminster parliament and establishing an independent government in Ireland. Despite Davitt's absorption in the land movement, he never lost sight of Irish self-government as an ultimate goal.

As Paul Bew points out, Parnell's approach was quite different. He believed that land reform and eventual peasant proprietorship might be won through constitutional means, and if so, it would remove the class barrier that prevented landlords supporting the Home Rule cause. In this way at least a proportion of the Irish landlord class would be available to the political movement.[21]

The Land League constantly reiterated its non-violent nature, and Davitt and others hotly denied any incitement to violence in their speeches.[22] Indeed, Parnell, in his evidence to the Special Commission on Parnellism and Crime, stressed Davitt's influence in discouraging violence within the movement.[23] Nevertheless, while he was deeply opposed to the spontaneous and undisciplined resort to violence that had characterised Ribbonism, Davitt's approach to the use of physical force was quite complex and he was not a pacifist. He believed, for example, in the right of individuals to carry a gun, which he did himself at times, even having to draw it to defend himself on several occasions. Clearly the Land League had to be presented as a peaceful mass movement. However, until his expulsion from the Supreme Council of the I.R.B., probably on 8 May 1880,[24] he was certainly aware of arms-smuggling and may have participated in it himself.[25] Viewing the landlord system as inherently violent, he appears to have had no moral qualms about opposing it with physical force; his objections to doing so were practical. It is unlikely that he believed the ultimate separation of Ireland and Britain could be won through peaceful means, a point raised by Parnell's response, 'And what next?', when Davitt had outlined a plan of secession from parliament to him in 1878.[26]

Moreover, as Parnell had appreciated in his cautious response to the Land League, it would prove very difficult for such a mass organisation to control the actions of its more hot-headed supporters. The League replaced and to an extent subsumed earlier Ribbon societies in the west, and it was inevitable that there would be some continuity in tactics. Even in the case of the moral pressure advocated for use against landlords and tenant farmers who rented evicted farms, there were evidently occasions when the line between boycotting and intimidation was narrow. Levels of violence rose significantly. During the period 1879–82 the mean number of agrarian murders rose to seventeen from a level of five per annum for the previous twenty-five years. Reported instances of lesser agrarian crime reached a peak in the last quarter of 1880 at more than twenty-five times the level in the same period of 1878.[27]

Growth of the Land League

In the autumn of 1879 the land movement began to spread beyond the western counties to other parts of Ireland, and increasingly existing tenant organisations affiliated to it. From the beginning it had attracted support from various social groups, but the extension into areas where larger farms predominated had certain implications for the movement. Indeed, one of the extraordinary aspects of the Land League was its success in attracting both large and small tenant farmers, labourers, graziers, and the rural bourgeoisie and clergy.[28] While this was a source of its strength, it also necessitated a certain papering-over the cracks of class conflict within the farming community in order to focus on opposition to the landlords, a fudge summarised in the Land League slogan, 'The Land for the People' (*which* people was never specified, apart from the fact that it was not to include the landlords).[29] For many of the small tenants of the west with whom Davitt identified, their holdings were too small to yield a living while paying any rent. Therefore their aim was owner-occupancy. The larger farmers and graziers, on the other hand, were able to pay rents, but in the face of economic decline they felt that their landlords should share more of the burden and accept rent reductions. As representatives of a rising Catholic elite, they were anxious not to see the social and economic position they had achieved in the post-Famine decades eroded by the depression. However, their interests and tactics were rather different to those of the small tenants of the west. Indeed, the point has been made that throughout Ireland Land League agitation was strongest in those regions where a dynamic grazier economy coexisted most closely with subsistence farming and rural poverty, thereby sharpening local class tensions.[30]

In theory, the procedure adopted by the Land League was that the tenants on an estate should combine to demand rent reductions; if this was refused, they should offer the landlord what they considered fair; if he disagreed with them, they should offer to submit the matter to arbitration. If their reduced rent was tendered and refused, they should hold on to it, and if they were evicted, no other tenant should take over the land, on pain of boycotting by the neighbourhood.[31] However, the practice varied widely, depending on local circumstances.[32] The radical wing of the League favoured an all-out rent strike, as first advocated by Fintan Lalor. However, increasingly the tactic adopted was to obstruct ejectments as far as possible in the courts and to follow a policy of payment at the very last moment, 'at the point of the bayonet', thus making life difficult for landlords but not running the risk of tenants actually losing their holdings. In the end the tenant would have to pay not only the rent but substantial legal costs as well, which the Land League normally bore. This was the tactic favoured by the larger tenants, and its adoption was the price of their support for the League. Therefore, while the League often adopted the rhetoric of the rent strike, the reality was that of 'rent at the point of the bayonet'. This was the 'sham' objected to so strongly by Anna Parnell.[33]

There were considerable tensions within the Land League between the smaller tillage farmers, particularly those in the west, and graziers. Graziers were at times excluded from the League, or boycotted or intimidated, in order to induce them not to take land that might otherwise be used for tillage. Another inherent conflict was between farmers and labourers. The Land League succeeded in attracting significant numbers of agricultural labourers to its banner, but despite support for their demands on the part of the neo-Fenians, including Davitt, any proposals for reform tended to come up against the interests of their tenant-farmer employers.[34] Davitt was concerned about the watering down of the organisation's initial radicalism by the influx of larger farmers, and he attempted to strengthen the hands of those who supported the small farmers and labourers within the Land League,[35] confiding to Devoy on 16 December 1880:

> There is a danger . . . of this class [larger farmers] and the priests coalescing and ousting the advanced men or gaining control of the whole thing and turning it against us. I am taking every precaution, however, against this Whig dodge. Already I have carried a neat constitution by a *coup de main* and on Tuesday next I intend to carry the election of an executive council of fifteen in whose hands the entire government will be placed. The Council will consist of six or seven M.P.s, and the remainder men like Brennan, Egan and myself.[36]

In his public writing Davitt sometimes tended to minimise such class differences, referring as he did to 'the Celtic peasantry of Ireland' as if it was an undifferentiated mass. While he was certainly conscious of the inherent class conflict within the farming community, he and others probably chose to downplay it in the interests of unity in what they viewed as the primary struggle against landlordism. Much of what he wrote at the time was propaganda for the League and journalism for an American readership. To emphasise class differences within the movement would not have served his purposes, since it was important that

Land League support remain united.[37] However, in the course of the Land League struggle it is clear that it was the larger tenants who benefited most. Paul Bew has suggested that Davitt's espousal of land nationalisation was in part a reaction of disgust towards such an outcome.[38] Both Davitt and Parnell were anxious in subsequent years that something be done to benefit farm labourers who had gained nothing from the land war.

Immediately following its foundation, the Land League received wide publicity through the government's prosecution of Davitt and two other activists, James Daly of Castlebar and James Bryce Killen, for speeches made at a meeting at Gurteen, County Sligo, on 2 November. Davitt had been released from Dartmoor in 1877 on a ticket-of-leave which ran until the end of his original sentence in 1884. This meant that in a case where he was found to be breaking the terms of his release, he could be reimprisoned without trial to serve the remainder of his sentence. However, this threat does not seem to have had any deterrent effect on him. In the event, the government chose not to revoke his ticket-of-leave, but to let him stand trial for sedition. From the government's point of view, the Sligo prosecutions were a mistake. They won the Land League publicity and sympathy at home and abroad, and the case, transferred to the Queen's Bench, was eventually dropped.

The bulk of the national organisational work of the Land League was carried out by Davitt, Brennan and Egan in the League's office at 39 Upper Sackville Street, Dublin. It involved arranging and attending meetings of the League and its executive, and conducting correspondence with branches around the country and with the press and public generally. They were unsalaried and theoretically part-time officers. Meetings of the executive were held once or twice weekly. On weekends Davitt would address Land League meetings in various parts of the country, encouraging and assisting in the formation of new branches. In addition, he had to earn his living, which he did through journalism, mainly for two American newspapers, John Boyle O'Reilly's *Boston Pilot* and Patrick Ford's *Irish World*. Within the executive, Egan was responsible for finance, Brennan for propaganda, and Davitt for organisation, with Parnell in charge of public policy. A. J. Kettle dealt with matters relating to agriculture and labour. It was Davitt who drafted the 'Appeal to the Irish Race', which served as the manifesto of the Land League, and the 'Suggestions on Organisation' to provide guidance on the setting up of Land League branches. Together with Brennan, he also drew up a form for gathering details on individual holdings, such as the size and value of the tenancy, whether the rent had been raised since 1848, the name of the landlord or agent, and so on. Davitt and his colleagues tried to keep the costs of administration down by employing as few paid staff as possible. The Land League grew very rapidly (Davitt estimated that by February 1881 it had about 200,000 members in 1,000 branches; while Samuel Clark has suggested that this may have been an exaggeration, he asserted that the number of Land League branches 'certainly exceeded five hundred').[39] With branches springing up around the country and contacts forged overseas, the resources of the office were at times overstretched.[40]

Support in the United States

Continued support from the Irish abroad was vital to the progress of the Land League's campaign. Early in 1880 Parnell and Dillon toured North America, gathering funds both for the League and for relief of distress in the west. However, it was felt necessary that someone from the parent organisation should oversee the setting up of an American body, and in May 1880 Davitt was sent to the U.S., Brennan assuming his responsibilities in the Dublin office. He arrived in New York on 18 May, in time to attend a convention established to form the Irish National Land and Industrial League of the United States, of which he was immediately elected secretary. He agreed to serve for as long as he remained in America, which turned out to be six months. His work was similar to that in Ireland. He had to establish a central office for the American League in New York and in addition, he undertook a twelve-week tour across the United States, ending in San Francisco. Davitt's role called for diplomatic skills in steering a course for the new organisation between the various warring factions in Irish-American nationalism. At the same time, he had to fight off an attack by traditional Fenians, Jeremiah O'Donovan Rossa and John O'Leary, who rejected the neo-Fenian approach and saw the Land League as a deviation from the 'real struggle'.

Two events occurred during this visit to America that had great significance for Davitt's personal life. The first was the death of his mother, Catherine Davitt, on 18 July. This caused him deep sorrow and remorse, in particular because he had been unable to fulfil his promise to bring her back to Ireland. The second was his meeting with Mary Yore, in Oakland, San Francisco, in September, at the end of a gruelling lecture tour during which he had suffered recurrent bouts of malaria. Mary was then eighteen years old; she had been orphaned in childhood and was living with her aunt, Mrs Mary Canning, an active participant in nationalist circles in Oakland. Davitt and Mary Yore were to marry in 1886.

The Land War at its Height

Davitt left for Ireland in November 1880 as the land war entered a new phase. The harvest had been a good one, but the League leaders were determined that the landlords would not take advantage of this to renew their claims on tenants for arrears. Boycotting was widespread, and despite efforts on the part of the leadership, cases of intimidation and reports of agrarian crimes were increasing. Just before Davitt's departure from America, Parnell and thirteen other Land League leaders were charged with criminal conspiracy. Davitt threw himself back into his old role, writing, organising and addressing League meetings. In December he presented an address to the people of Ulster, which was aimed at strengthening the Land League in the north, following it up with a series of meetings at venues in northern counties.

By the time Davitt returned from America government and landlord resistance was beginning to build up against the Land League. In December 1880 a landlord body, the Property Defence Association, had been formed. A propaganda war emphasised the rise in agrarian crime, and the Chief Secretary, W. E. Forster, was urging the government to suspend *habeas corpus*, in which case, Davitt believed, 'the whole movement would be crushed in a month and universal confusion would reign'.[41] Davitt knew he was in danger of reimprisonment and contemplated fleeing to Paris, but in the meantime he urged self-discipline and better organisation on the movement. He was particularly vehement in his condemnation of outrages on people and animals, mutilation of livestock being a frequent feature of the land war. Anxious to take the struggle to a more political level, he urged branches to concentrate on putting forward candidates for the board of guardians elections the following March, while keeping up their peaceful struggle against landlords. He argued that if Irish tenants maintained their pressure on the government, they would ultimately be victorious. Privately, however, he still feared the influx of moderates into the League, who would be prepared to compromise.

After two months of proceedings the conspiracy charges against the Land League leaders failed when the jury was unable to reach a verdict. However, the Dublin Castle administration used the difficulty of obtaining convictions to support its argument for the suspension of *habeas corpus.*

The new parliamentary session began on 6 January 1881 with a Queen's Speech promising both coercive and remedial measures. One of these would provide for an increase in Dublin Castle's police powers, while the other offered land reform. The Parnellites at Westminster fought the Protection of Person and Property Bill with unprecedented levels of obstruction. At the same time the leaders of the Land League had to work out strategies for meeting the attempts to suppress their movement that were clearly in the offing. Davitt and Dillon urged that Parnell should go to America to collect funds. Kettle, however, suggested a more radical policy. The core of it consisted of a plan whereby, on the day the coercion bill became law, the parliamentary party should withdraw from Westminster, return to Ireland and declare a general strike against rent.[42] This was seen as a particularly auspicious time to take a stand against the government, as the Boers had just declared war against Britain. Davitt later recalled that Parnell was not opposed to such a policy, but that several of his influential colleagues were strongly against it, and no decision was reached.[43]

Another means of responding to the situation was suggested by Davitt. At a meeting of the League executive on 26 January 1881 to discuss how to provide for the possibility that the entire leadership might shortly be arrested, he proposed the formation of a Ladies' Land League, which would be in a position to take over the work. An American Ladies' Land League had been founded by Fanny Parnell in the previous October while Davitt was in the U.S., and during the summer both she and her sister Anna had worked in the American League offices in New York. In a letter to the *Nation* on 1 January, Fanny had advocated the formation of an Irish equivalent but had met with little response.

Davitt's proposal, he later recalled, 'was laughed at by all except Mr Egan and myself, and vehemently opposed by Messrs Parnell, Dillon, and Brennan, who feared we would invite public ridicule in appearing to put women forward in places of danger'.[44] Eventually, however, the opponents reluctantly agreed to give their 'passive assent to what they dreaded would be a most dangerous experiment'.[45] The Ladies' Land League, founded in January 1881, was to become the first political organisation led and run by women in Ireland.

Early in 1881 the government decided to move against Davitt, and on 3 February he was arrested as he was crossing Carlisle (O'Connell) Bridge in Dublin, brought to London under heavy guard and committed to Millbank prison in London. The public reaction was immediate. In Westminster, such was the anger and exasperation of the Irish M.P.s that thirty-six of them were expelled from the house for the rest of the sitting. Once more, the question of withdrawal from parliament was discussed, only to be rejected again.

Owing to his public status, Davitt's treatment was much better than during his first term in prison.[46] There was widespread concern about the possible effect that incarceration might have on his health. He was moved almost immediately to Portland prison in Dorset, where he was allowed to stay in the prison infirmary and permitted a special diet. An enlightened and humane prison governor allowed him to work in the infirmary garden, where he developed a keen interest in horticulture. He was allowed any books he requested, apart from those on current affairs or newspapers, provided with writing materials and received more visitors and letters than his status as a third-degree prisoner would normally have allowed. Thus he was able to write the material on which his first book, *Leaves from a Prison Diary*, was based.[47] Nevertheless, the terms of his imprisonment were considerably harsher than those under which the other Land League leaders were to be held in Kilmainham.

With Davitt in jail, Egan in Paris (having smuggled out the League's funds to prevent their seizure), and the imprisonment of Harris, Dillon, Brennan and Kettle which followed, the radical leadership of the League was removed. A certain degree of chaos in the League's offices resulted. More importantly, although these men at the core of the movement were viewed as dangerous radicals by the government and were certainly very far to the left of the Home Rule Party generally, they had served an important role in keeping the wilder spirits, who trusted them, in check. In their absence, it was much more likely that a wedge could be driven between the right and left wings of the League by the provisions of the 1881 land bill, announced in April, with the right favouring a compromise settlement, far short of the Land League's demand of peasant proprietorship, and the disaffected supporters on the left veering toward violence. Therefore, while on a personal level Davitt's imprisonment offered him a time for rest and fruitful thought, for the movement he had built it was a very serious blow.

Gladstone introduced his new land bill on 7 April 1881. What it offered was essentially the 'three Fs', which had been the demand of moderate land reformers before the advent of the Land League. However, the measure would not provide any assistance to leaseholders or tenants in arrears. Nor did it permit the new land courts set up under the act to take any account of those tenants whose rents had been too high, perhaps for decades. From the radicals' point of view, the problem was that many, perhaps most, tenants would settle for what they could get, rather than pressing on for the ultimate goal of ownership. And yet, from the government's and the landlords' points of view, the legislation was revolutionary, as it provided for state intervention in the contract between landlord and tenant and represented a tacit admission on the part of Gladstone and his government that the tenants needed to be protected against their landlords.

Years later, in *The Fall of Feudalism in Ireland*, Davitt was to describe the act as 'a work of Mr Gladstone's genius as a statesman', 'a semi-revolutionary scheme . . . which struck a mortal blow at Irish landlordism and doomed it to abolition'.[48] At the time, however, the response of Parnell and his followers was to criticise the measure as insufficient, without completely dismissing it, and it was decided to 'test the act' with a number of selected cases.

In October 1881 Parnell and other leaders were imprisoned in Kilmainham jail. They responded almost immediately by proclaiming a rent strike. Davitt's name was among the signatories of the manifesto, but he could not be consulted and probably would have refused to sign it, believing as he did that the timing was misjudged. In the event, the 'No Rent Manifesto' was a failure, simply giving Forster an excuse to suppress the League. Its work, however, was, as planned by Davitt, taken over by the Ladies' Land League.

The Ladies' Land League

The misgivings of the Land League leaders were not the only opposition the Ladies' Land League had to face. Archbishop McCabe of Dublin, already hostile to the Land League, claimed that the organisation was asking 'the daughters of our Catholic people . . . to jeopardise the modesty of their sex and the dignity of their womanhood' by participation.[49] Newspapers, including the *Connaught Telegraph* and the *Belfast News-Letter* (the latter generally opposed to the Land League), criticised the call to women to leave their 'natural' habitat of the home. While Davitt shared a prevailing belief in the importance of women's role in the home, this did not prevent him from urging that they be given a place in the land struggle, arguing that the fight to save the homes of Ireland was theirs too. If they were sent to prison, it would turn world public opinion against the authorities. His approach to this question may have been influenced by his background and experience. In peasant societies women were traditionally to the fore in popular protests, and there was a custom that it was the women's responsibility to preserve the home.[50] Both from his rural background and his having grown up in an industrial environment where women typically worked outside the home, Davitt may have had a different approach than some of his colleagues. Many women were already involved in the Land League, either as heads of households (usually through widowhood) or by their participation in boycotting and eviction protests, where they were frequently the target of police violence.[51] The question was not whether to allow them to participate at all, as they were already active at a grassroots level; it was whether to allow them to assume leadership roles.[52] By contrast, the Fenian movement, from which several Land League leaders, including Davitt, had come, was very masculine in character, excluding women, by its emphasis on militarism, from any role other than passive support.[53]

The difference, however, reflected a wider divergence over the participation of women in public life. Many of the leaders of Irish nationalism, John Dillon and John Redmond among them, were later to prove hostile to the introduction of women's suffrage (Dillon predicting that it would 'be the ruin of our western civilisation').[54] Davitt, on the other hand, was in favour of it, signing a memorial in 1905 urging members of the Irish Parliamentary Party to support the Women's Suffrage Bill then before the House of Commons.[55]

On the establishment of the Ladies' Land League, Anna Parnell, sister of Charles Stewart Parnell, was appointed general secretary and the new organisation was provided with an office in the headquarters of the Land League in Upper Sackville Street, Dublin. Nevertheless, from the first, as she recounted in *The Tale of a Great Sham*, the women faced both passive and active opposition from their male colleagues. Their role within the movement and the work they were expected to undertake were never explained to them, they were given very limited access to records, and they were subjected to constant criticism. Despite this, the Ladies' Land League established an important role for itself, in fact extending the work of the Land League.[56] It provided assistance to evicted tenants and those facing eviction, making available prefabricated houses where necessary, supplying food and other aid to prisoners and supporting their families. Within its first year the new organisation had over 400 branches throughout the country. Its leaders addressed public meetings, and the new League was able to maintain the publication and distribution of *United Ireland* while William O'Brien, the paper's editor, was in prison. A further venture about which Davitt was particularly enthusiastic was the establishment of weekly clubs for children

which introduced them to Irish history, 'so that the next generation of Irishmen shall know something about their own
country'.[57] When the Land League was proclaimed in October
1881, the Ladies' Land League assumed the leadership of the
land war, until its own suppression in December and the arrest of
some of its members.

The membership of the Ladies' Land League tended to be
more urban and more middle class than its male counterpart,
though there was a substantial rural membership too. It was also
more radical. Anna Parnell objected strongly to the policy of 'rent
at the point of a bayonet', believing that it involved the Land
League in unnecessary expenses that would end up in the
landlord's pocket without doing him any real harm. She and her
associates were, moreover, opposed to testing the 1881 act,
believing that it was insufficient to meet the needs of farmers.
When, early in 1882, the imprisoned Land League leaders
ordered the women to call off the 'no rent' campaign, they were
ignored, as it was felt that, however badly timed its announcement
had been, to change policy so abruptly would be equally harmful.
Parnell appears to have become alarmed at the radicalism of the
women and determined, on his release in May 1882, to bring
their organisation to an end. In fact, however, there seems to have
been some tacit recognition of their administrative ability,
because it was proposed that they should continue to handle
dealings with tenants while taking orders from the Land League
leadership. In the end, amid much rancour, the Ladies' Land
League was wound up in August 1882.

The first phase of the land war was brought to a close
following the conclusion of the 'Kilmainham Treaty' in May 1882.
This was an informal agreement between Parnell and Gladstone
that the land war would be ended in exchange for legislation that
would include leaseholders in the terms of the 1881 Land Act; the
introduction of measures to protect tenants with heavy arrears in
rent; and the release of Land League prisoners. Accordingly, after
fifteen months in Portland prison, Davitt was released on 6 May
1882, Parnell and Dillon travelling to Dorset to meet him. On the
train to London Parnell accused the women of having done great
harm to the movement, Davitt commenting sardonically: 'The
harm is evident in the fall of Forster and in the dropping of

coercion and in our release.'[58] However, despite the fact that he
continued to believe that the dissolution of the Ladies' Land
League was a great mistake, he did not intervene to prevent it,
perhaps because in the long run their radicalism might have
threatened to split the movement along class lines.[59]

Davitt's opinion of the Ladies' Land League remained positive
in 1904, when he wrote *The Fall of Feudalism in Ireland*. He recognised that they had built an efficient organisation and had kept
the Land League movement alive, whereas with the arrest of its
leaders, 'there was no head and had it been left to itself then it
would have broken up'.[60] He tended to overstate the militancy of
the women, implying that they turned a blind eye to agrarian
violence,[61] and an angry Anna Parnell denounced his account as
containing several 'wanton, malicious and impudent libels'
concerning her.[62] Nevertheless, Davitt would have shared much of
their social radicalism, and it was unfortunate for them that
having been imprisoned the day after the formation of the organisation, he was unable to provide what might otherwise have been
an important link with the Land League leadership. As it turned
out, the participation of women seems to have incurred so great a
degree of hostility that they were explicitly excluded from
membership of the Land League's successor, the Irish National
League.

Davitt and the Land War

Davitt's contribution to the land campaign was crucial. In the
first place, he embodied in his own person some of the grievances
the Irish tenants suffered. He had experienced eviction; he had
lived as an Irish emigrant; he had suffered the loss of an arm as an
indirect result of eviction and emigration; he had served a long
prison sentence in the cause of militant republicanism. Thus he
was able to gain their sympathy and trust in mobilising the tenant
farmers behind the movement. In speeches throughout the
country and in his journalism he explained the ideas of the new
organisation that he and his associates had created. During much
of the land struggle, moreover, he was sending regular articles to
the Irish-American journals to explain the issues to the Irish
communities there and to seek their support. He set up the
headquarters of the Irish and American sections of the Land

League, and, perhaps most importantly, his ideas, which helped to infuse both Fenianism and trade union tactics into the land movement, were influential in the formulation of its policies. He did not function alone, and the roles of other leaders, such as Matthew Harris, James Daly, Thomas Brennan and Andrew Kettle, have frequently been overlooked. Nevertheless, it is fair to say that the most significant individual contribution in shaping the Land League as a movement was Davitt's.

3

AFTER THE LAND LEAGUE, 1882–91

By May 1882, with the Land League suppressed and not to be revived, Davitt's leadership of land agitation was ended. Nevertheless, he was to remain an important figure in Anglo-Irish politics, his interests broadening in the 1880s to include a campaign for land nationalisation, involvement in the British and Irish labour movements, and preparation of the defence for the Irish nationalist leaders in the Special Commission on Parnellism and Crime.

The 'Kilmainham Treaty'

Under the terms of the 'Kilmainham Treaty', concluded in April 1882, the imprisoned Home Rule M.P.s were released on 2 May and Davitt four days later. Gladstone undertook that the government would introduce a substantial measure of relief for small tenants in arrears, who had been left out of the provisions of the 1881 Land Act. On his side, Parnell was to use his influence to end the disorder in the countryside and to co-operate with the Liberal Party.

The so-called 'treaty' brought some significant achievements. Within a few months Gladstone introduced legislation which settled the arrears of some 130,000 of the most needy tenants, thus allowing them to apply to the land courts set up under the 1881 Land Act in order to have their rents judicially fixed.[1] The 1881 act was followed up in 1885 by the Ashbourne Land Act, brought in by Lord Salisbury's Conservative administration in 1885, which for the first time provided for the advance by the state of all of the purchase money of a holding, instead of only a portion of it. It is in this sense that the Kilmainham agreement may be seen as moving on the process towards peasant proprietorship. However, there was a price to pay, in the form of the abandonment of the agrarian struggle. The Ladies' Land League was rapidly brought to an end, and the Land League, proclaimed in October 1881, was not revived. For Parnell, this was a logical step. He had achieved as much as he felt to be possible at the time in the direction of agrarian legislation, and he now sought to turn his full attention to the parliamentary struggle for Home Rule.

For Davitt, though, abandonment of the land struggle was a bitter blow. In his eyes, the battle had been called off when victory was almost in sight. He saw the Land League as having been organised to bring about the abolition of landlordism, and until that was accomplished there could be no alliance between the Irish people and the Liberal Party.[2] Had he been less loyal to Parnell and to the long-term aims of Irish nationalism, he might have attempted a rupture with the parliamentarians and, together with Dillon, Brennan, Harris and other agrarian radicals, carried on the struggle against landlordism. However, despite his evident disappointment, he does not seem to have contemplated such a move. His position was weakened, moreover, by his espousal of land nationalisation, which won very little support in Ireland or among Irish-Americans.

Land Nationalisation

Davitt had used the fifteen months in Portland Prison, from February 1881 to May 1882, to draft his first book, *Leaves from a Prison Diary, or Lectures to a 'Solitary' Audience.*[3] This is a collection of thirty-four essays or 'lectures' on a variety of themes. The first volume consists in the main of a description and analysis of the prisoners amongst whom he found himself during this and his previous prison terms. The second covers a range of social issues, providing the most comprehensive and systematic source of Davitt's social thought at this time. Among the issues discussed are the importance of education and recreation in preventing crime; the causes of poverty and suggestions for its prevention; the organisation of labour; a proposal to introduce 'state socialism'; and a critique of British government in Ireland.

Central to Davitt's programme was state ownership of land. The book contained his first open espousal of the idea of land nationalisation, although he told the Parnell Commission that he had been a land nationaliser before he had met Henry George in 1880.[4] Nor was the idea of land nationalisation entirely new: it was already current among radical and socialist groups from at least the early 1870s.[5]

Nevertheless, there is no doubt that Davitt was influenced by George's book, *Progress and Poverty*, first published in 1879 in the U.S. and a year later in Britain. It traced the evils associated with an unequal distribution of wealth to the existence of private property in land. George developed an interest in the Irish land question, visited Ireland four times during the 1880s, and wrote his own study of *The Irish Land Question*, published in March 1881. In this pamphlet George started from the slogan of the Land League, 'The Land of Ireland for the People of Ireland' and asked what that meant. Obviously it signified more than rent reductions, but it also, he argued, meant more than peasant proprietorship, or, as he put it, 'that the State shall buy the land from one class and sell it to another class'.[6] It suggested that the land should be resumed by the whole people, and that 'To propose to pay the landlords for it is to deny the right of the people to it.'[7] Land, he continued, reiterating the central point of *Progress and Poverty*, is a different kind of commodity to any other because, on the one hand, it does not decay, and, on the other, it is the basic source of livelihood from generation to generation: 'The right to possess and to pass on the ownership of things that in their nature decay and soon cease to be is a very different thing from the right to possess and to pass on the ownership of that which does not decay but from which each successive generation must live.'[8] His solution was to 'divert the rent which now flows into the pockets of landlords into the common treasury of the whole people. It is not possible to so divide up the land of Ireland so as to give each family, still less each individual, an equal share . . . But it is possible to equally divide the rent or, what amounts to the same thing, to apply it to purposes of common benefit.'[9] This he would do by means of taxing land 'up to its full value'.

The goal espoused by the Land League had been peasant proprietorship, but following Henry George, Davitt now reinterpreted the slogan 'The Land for the People' in a new way. He held that peasant proprietorship would be insufficient, as it 'will not destroy, it will only extend the absolute ownership of land: *an ownership which will always be in the market for purchase and re-consolidation into large estates*'.[10] He further asked why the state should transform tenants into proprietors , giving them land that rightly belonged to all: 'By what right are the public funds or the public credit to be utilised for the benefit of a section of the community merely?'[11] He foresaw correctly that the provision of state aid for tenants to buy out their holdings would create a very immobile land system, and since state assistance would only be extended to the first buyer, the labourers would be practically excluded 'from all hope of ever being able to elevate themselves from their present degraded condition to anything better in connection with the land'.[12]

On 6 June, just a month after his release, Davitt announced his support for the policy of land nationalisation, and he soon joined Henry George in a series of public meetings on the subject in Britain. There was considerable interest and some sympathy for their ideas, and they were assisted by the influential New York paper, the *Irish World*, whose owner, Patrick Ford, was also a supporter of land nationalisation.

In the context of the time, Davitt's programme was utopian and probably impracticable. However, it reflects a view that not only embraced tenant farmers but also took account of the interests of wider sectors of society, including agricultural labourers and urban workers. It met with implacable opposition on the part of most of the Irish Parliamentary Party, which was increasingly identifying 'the nation' with the Irish tenant farming interest, which formed the backbone of its support. Davitt's efforts to promote it were viewed as a serious matter owing to his popularity and influence among nationalists and agrarian reformers. At a time when Parnell was engaged in winding down the Land League and Davitt had good reason to be disgruntled, his land nationalisation campaign was perceived by some as a challenge to Parnell's leadership. For his part, Parnell was hostile to the programme from the first, castigating it in 1884 as 'a chaotic socialist experiment'.[13]

The Irish National League

Isolated by his imprisonment from political developments, Davitt's release had come as a surprise to him. He did not hear the terms of the 'Kilmainham Treaty' until he was on the train with Parnell, Dillon and O'Kelly, who had travelled to Portland to meet him. On the following morning in London they received the news that Lord Frederick Cavendish, the new Chief Secretary, and the Under-Secretary, Thomas Henry Burke, had been assassinated in Phoenix Park in Dublin on the evening of the previous day. They were shocked by the murders, Davitt drafting a manifesto condemning them, which was signed by Parnell and Dillon. For Davitt, it was to mark his final break with the Fenians. On 11 May he had an interview with Howard Vincent, director of the C.I.D., in which he declared that he was no longer a Fenian, that his own life was in danger, and that he believed the assassination to be the work of 'a few desperate ruffians' who were still in Dublin.[14]

Davitt spent June and July of 1882 in America on a lecture tour. On his return to London, on 3 August he presented Parnell with a plan for a new organisation to be called 'The National Land and Industrial Union of Ireland'.[15] This was to be a democratic body, with an elected leadership and with a much wider social role than had the Land League, embracing social, industrial, educational and political reform. Its main aim would be 'the complete abolition of the landlord system', which, Davitt hoped, would be replaced by land nationalisation. But it would also be concerned with improving the conditions of agricultural labourers, provision of better housing, a revival of manufacturing industries, and the establishment of a co-operative land and labour association with a capital of £1 million, to be spent on purchasing unoccupied and waste land on which to settle labourers and evicted tenants. A network of Mechanics' Institutes would be established to improve the provision of education to the labouring classes and to encourage the study of Irish literature and language. The political programme would include repeal of the Act of Union, followed by national self-government, and, pending its attainment, improved parliamentary representation, financial assistance for Home Rule M.P.s, and local government reform.

Parnell, however, did not want a revived Land League, preferring to concentrate on the political campaign. He argued that in the face of new coercion (introduced in response to the Phoenix Park murders) the country needed a rest from agitation. Davitt's comment in *The Fall of Feudalism* expresses his sense of disappointment:

It was the vital turning point in Mr Parnell's career, and he unfortunately turned in the wrong direction. He had hitherto been in everything but name a revolutionary reformer, and had won many triumphs at the head of the most powerful organisation any Irish leader had at his back for a century. He now resolved to surrender the Land League and to enter the new stage of his political fortunes as an opportunist statesman.[16]

Nevertheless, Parnell did agree to participate in the establishment of the Irish Labour and Industrial Union, formed in August 1882, with the more limited aims of ameliorating the position of agricultural labourers through providing them with access to land, the extension of the franchise to them, and the encouragement of Irish industries to provide alternative employment for them. It also aimed at harmonising their interests with those of urban workers, and Parnell urged them to avoid conflict with farmers. Its committee included some of the old Land League core—Davitt, Dillon and Matthew Harris.

Further negotiations led to a meeting at Avondale, Parnell's family home, on 13 September, attended by Davitt, Dillon, Brennan and Parnell, at which it was agreed to set up a new national organisation, the Irish National League. The new body was launched at a conference on 17 October 1882. It was in a sense a successor organisation to both the Land League and the Home Rule League. Its programme encompassed an impressive range of social and political reforms[17] and included a few of Davitt's proposals. However, it was to be dominated by a central clique, loyal to Parnell, socially conservative and oriented toward parliamentary rather than popular politics, resulting in a containment of the movement's earlier social radicalism. At the Avondale meeting Davitt had undertaken not to raise the question of land nationalisation. These developments, as he was later to write, brought about

> the complete eclipse, by a purely parliamentary substitute, of what had been a semi-revolutionary organisation . . . the overthrow of a movement and the enthronement of a man.[18]

Amid much speculation, Dillon announced his resignation from Irish politics 'for the next few years' on health grounds. Patrick Egan, the treasurer of the Land League, also resigned, in order to devote more time to his business; shortly afterwards he emigrated to America. Brennan too left for the United States. None of them made any public criticism of Parnell or his leadership, but their withdrawal raised speculation about the 'Kilmainham Treaty' and the abandonment of the land agitation. Davitt did not openly challenge the new organisation, but he did not like it. The years from 1882 to 1885 saw attempts to improve discipline in the Irish Parliamentary Party. Home Rule M.P.s were to be paid from a parliamentary fund and were therefore more amenable to a party whip. In 1885 the local organisations were welded into a formal convention structure which gave the central authority in Dublin influence over nominations. All this was accompanied by what Davitt saw as a growing adulation of Parnell. 'Parnellism', he was later to relate,

> triumphed completely in the constitution of the governing body of the National League. This body was made almost exclusively pro-Parnellite, as against the extreme men who had worked loyally with Mr Parnell in the Land League, but who were not prepared to look upon the name of Parnellite as a substitute for nationalist, either in practice or in principle, or to invest him, or any individual, with arbitrary power.[19]

As Parnell himself largely confined his activities to Britain in 1883–4, a good deal of the management of the National League in Ireland was carried on by Healy, Harrington and other lieutenants using his name to silence opposition.

Neither evictions nor rural unrest ended with the demise of the Land League. Indeed, coercion on the government side was matched by a dynamite campaign launched by the physical-force wing of Irish-American nationalism. While Davitt had no hesitation in condemning the bombings, he equally denounced perceived injustices on the part of the forces of the law, such as the execution of three men for the Maamtrasna murders in 1882, although one of them was widely believed to have had nothing to do with the crime.[20]

As a result of what were considered seditious speeches, Davitt was imprisoned once again—for the last time, as it happened—in February 1883, in the Richmond Bridewell. The sentence was for six months, of which he served four, being released in June. Serving alongside him was T. M. Healy, at this time a leading figure in the more conservative 'party within a party', a parliamentarian rather than a land reformer, whereas Davitt was still trying to urge a more radical policy on the National League leadership. Nevertheless, the two men seem to have got along quite well, Davitt teaching Healy Irish.

In consideration of the anti-Irish feeling in Britain that resulted from the 'dynamite campaign' of 1883–8, Davitt approached Parnell early in 1883 with the suggestion of broadening out the Irish Party's programme to encompass reforming legislation for Britain. This, he urged, would attract British working-class sympathy and help to create a joint platform with the Radicals. Parnell's response was that the Irish electorate would not understand it, though this may also have reflected Parnell's own social conservatism. In fact, although there was logic in the proposals, as the Radicals up to this point had been consistently friendly towards Irish reform, there would have been considerable opposition within the nationalist coalition to closer relations with them.

Support for Indian Nationalism

At this time several of the Irish leaders were conscious of the growing sense of Indian grievance at India's treatment within the British Empire. Indian political organisation had emerged with the formation of the British Indian Association in 1851 and the establishment of the Bombay Association the following year. In the 1850s and 1860s the Indian cause won the support of English Radicals such as Joseph Hume and John Bright, and when the obstructionist wing of the Home Rule Party came to the fore in the late 1870s, some of its members took an interest in Indian issues too. Foremost among these, as also in the case of the Boers, was F. H. O'Donnell, who declared that:

> English tyranny in Ireland was only part of that general system of the exploitation of suffering humanity which made the British Empire a veritable slave empire . . . Parliamentary agitation would not be very effective until the Irish people, crushed down under their present tyranny, effected a coalition with the oppressed natives of India and other British dependencies, and all regarded England as the common enemy.[21]

One of the founders of the Bombay Association, Dadabhai Naoroji, moved to Britain in 1855 to promote the Indian cause there.[22] He founded the London Indian Society to bring together Englishmen and Indians of all political hues. It was through F. H. O'Donnell that he met Parnell and Davitt, and in 1878 the idea was first broached by prominent Indians living in Britain that Ireland should elect an Indian representative to speak for India in the House of Commons, and that Indian nationalists would, in turn, endorse Irish policies. In 1883, with the wind taken out of the sails of the Irish Party by the terms of the 'Kilmainham Treaty', and with a continuation of repression of political activity in Ireland, Davitt included campaigning for Indian rights as one of the measures he advocated to broaden the scope of the party's programme. He urged that apart from the one pressing issue of better housing for Irish agricultural labourers, all Irish business should be abandoned for a session or two by the Irish M.P.s. Instead they should concentrate on English, Scottish and Welsh reforms, both social and political. This was aimed at winning wider public support for the Irish cause, and it would link the Irish struggle with a class struggle against privilege. In addition, the programme would include Imperial issues:

> It was also suggested that a seat might be found in Ireland for Mr Dadabhai Naoroje, a thoroughly representative Indian gentleman residing in London, and well known to Mr Parnell and others of us. Ireland would thus have the honour of giving a direct voice in the House of Commons to countless millions of British subjects who were ruled despotically and taxed without votes.[23]

While Parnell was 'very much "taken" at first' with the proposal, he later rejected it, expressing the fear that 'it would not be clearly understood in Ireland and might lead to trouble within the Party'.[24] Naoroji was eventually to win a seat for the Liberal Party in Central Finsbury in 1892, and Irish members, O'Donnell, Justin McCarthy and Joseph Biggar in particular, took an active part in asking questions on Indian policy in the House of Commons. Once Home Rule for Ireland appeared a possibility, it was seen as pointless to attempt to have Indian candidates elected to what might shortly be a separate parliament. Mary Cumpston has suggested that 'it was unfortunate . . . that some of

the warmest friends of India in the House were the Irish representatives', because the Irish had so infuriated the other members of
parliament by obstruction that 'the association of Indian nationalism with Irish torment' did it harm.[25] Although it might be argued
that the association also helped to bring Indian grievances rapidly
to public attention, it may have been a consideration of this sort
that led Davitt to refuse an invitation to preside at the Indian
National Congress of 1894 in Madras, on the grounds that 'his
presence would be too serious a risk for Congress to take'.[26]

    Davitt spent the first half of 1885 abroad, recovering his
health. Starting in France in early January, he moved to Italy,
where he interviewed Lojus Kossuth, 'one of my favourite heroes
when doing my boyhood reading'.[27] Kossuth, leader of the
Hungarian uprising in 1848, had been settled in Turin for many
years. Now aged eighty-two, he rarely received visitors, but he and
Davitt spent an afternoon discussing European social and political
affairs, Kossuth remarking as his guest took his leave: 'No matter
what happens, my friend, you and I will do our duty.' Davitt
travelled on to Palestine and Egypt in April, visiting holy sites and
trekking through the countryside on horseback. In May he
returned via Malta to Italy, Switzerland and Germany. Although
he had been briefly in France in 1879, this was his first extended
encounter with Europe and the Middle East.

British Radicals and the Irish Question

    By the 1880s the Liberal Party was deeply divided between the
more aristocratic Whigs and the Radicals, the latter generally
more favourable towards reform and more sympathetic towards
Irish demands. A sensible course of action for the Irish Party
leaders would seem to have been efforts to win over the Radicals
to joint action, as Davitt had suggested in 1883. However, not only
did the Irish Party fail to follow this course, but, on the contrary,
the 1880s saw divisions widening between the two groups. The
Irish were resentful of Radical support for the Liberals' coercion
measures. Some of them may even have held prejudices against
the Radicals' middle-class links with industry and trade.[28] A difference first emerged in 1880, with attempts by the reformer and
social thinker Charles Bradlaugh to gain admission to parliament,
having been returned for Northampton. Bitter opposition arose,

on the grounds that Bradlaugh was a publicly declared atheist. The Irish nationalists were divided on the issue: some, such as O'Donnell and Healy, conscious of their clerical support, were prominent in the attack, whereas others supported Bradlaugh, who had been a consistent upholder of the Irish cause. The controversy continued intermittently until 1886, when Bradlaugh was finally allowed to take his seat. Parnell, initially in favour of Bradlaugh's admission, later changed his mind. Davitt supported Bradlaugh's right to attend the house on the grounds that he had been democratically elected, but he was not a member of parliament and therefore did not have any say in the matter.[29]

The breach widened following the failure of a proposal by the then Radical Joseph Chamberlain for a reform of local government that would give Ireland a greater measure of administrative autonomy. The Home Rule Party eventually distanced itself from the scheme, and a planned visit to Ireland by Chamberlain and his Radical colleague Charles Dilke in 1885 was abandoned after being sharply attacked in the Irish National League's newspaper, *United Ireland*, and by Timothy Healy. Although he did not for a moment see local government reform as a substitute for Home Rule, Davitt nonetheless deplored the hostile reception threatened to the two English politicians should they come to Ireland, pointing out in *The Fall of Feudalism* that while it undoubtedly seemed 'very warlike and valiant in Dublin at the time', it was to have serious consequences later 'in reducing Mr Gladstone's subsequent majority in the House of Commons low enough to defeat his Home Rule Bill'.[30]

Davitt's political views were to the left of the constitutional movement. His natural political allies were the Radicals. Therefore he could only view with horror Parnell's flirtation with the Conservative Party in 1885, in which he urged the Irish in Britain to vote against the Liberals and Radicals, following hints from Randolph Churchill of Conservative support for Home Rule. In the event, some important reform legislation was passed for Ireland by the Conservative government. The Ashbourne Land Act provided for the purchase of holdings by tenants with loans extended by the Land Commission. Davitt's response was to denounce it as a 'landlord relief bill'.[31] In December Herbert Gladstone flew the famous 'Hawarden kite', when he informed journalists that his father was about to declare himself in favour of Home Rule; the Irish Party's swing to the Liberals thereafter accelerated.

The Plan of Campaign

The autumn of 1886 saw the announcement of the Plan of Campaign in Ireland. With a continued downward trend in agricultural prices, the rents fixed by the land courts were soon felt to be too high. A Tenants' Relief Bill to meet the situation was proposed by Parnell but was defeated in late September, and the Irish leaders were under great pressure from the country to undertake some action or face localised independent protest.[32] On 16 October the Plan was launched by Harrington, Dillon and O'Brien in the pages of *United Ireland*, in an effort to force rent abatements on landlords. The Plan was a return to the rent strike tactic of the 'No Rent Manifesto'. Under its provisions, tenants on estates where rents were considered excessive would seek an abatement. If the landlord or agent refused, they were to pay what they considered a fair rent into a campaign fund which would be used to pursue their case. Evicted tenants would be supported from the fund, negotiations with the landlord would be carried out by an estate committee, and any breaches of discipline would be dealt with by boycotting.

It must have come as a disappointment to many of his former colleagues in the Land League struggles that Davitt did not participate in the Plan. He had been in the United States in the autumn and winter of 1886, explaining to an American audience the Irish Party's rapprochement with the Liberals over the campaign for Home Rule. On his return early in 1887, Parnell urged him not to support the Plan. He told Davitt that he had not been consulted about the agitation[33] and argued that such a movement at this point would jeopardise Gladstone's chance of winning the next election, pointing out that since the 'Grand Old Man' was the only one likely to achieve Home Rule for Ireland, it would be folly to put obstacles in his way. A further consideration for Parnell, though not one he confided to Davitt, was that the conditions of the 'Kilmainham Treaty' bound him to avoid any participation in further land agitation under a Liberal government.[34] Davitt was convinced by Parnell's case and followed him initially in holding aloof from the Plan, although clearly he sympathised strongly with it. Nevertheless, he helped to raise funds for relief of tenants and was present to address the gathering to protest the evictions at Bodyke in County Clare in 1887. He was outspoken in his criticism of the papal rescript of 20 April 1888, which condemned the Plan of Campaign. In a speech on 27 April in Bray he declared that 'he never intended for one moment to obey the rescript, and he was pretty certain that the same might be said of ninety-nine out of every hundred lay Nationalist Catholics in Ireland'. He continued that 'the Irish people owed it to their own political and intellectual manhood, to their spirit of national independence, and, above all, to their Protestant fellow-country-men, to withstand every semblance of political dictation, interference, or direction on the part of Rome in their national and secular affairs'.[35]

By 1889, with Dillon abroad raising finances for the Plan of Campaign, O'Brien facing imprisonment, and the landlords fighting back through a syndicate supported by the Conservative Chief Secretary, Arthur Balfour, the Plan was in crisis. The cost of maintaining evicted tenants was running at around £20,000 per annum, and the funds would shortly run out. Finally, Parnell agreed to lend his name to the formation of a Tenants' Defence Association, set up in October to raise support for a continuation of the Plan. Davitt, who had urged the need for such an initiative on Parnell, became a member of its council.

The Special Commission on Parnellism and Crime

With the Plan scarcely under way, in an attempt to damage the relationship between the Irish Party and the Liberals, *The Times* published a series of articles, under the heading 'Parnellism and Crime', which appeared from March to December 1887. These attempted to link Parnell and his associates with crime, including complicity in the Phoenix Park murders, a claim that the paper supported by the use of forged documents. After several demands by Parnell for a parliamentary inquiry, the government established an official commission charged not so much with examining the newspaper's allegations as with investigating crime in Ireland and whether the Irish political movement had any hand in instigating it. Davitt threw himself into preparing the Irish nationalists' defence and efforts to expose and frustrate what he saw as a plot to discredit the Home Rule movement.[36] He gave evidence to the commission over seven days; his submission was later printed in book form.[37] In the event, the commission, which sat 128 times between October 1888 and November 1889, was unable to establish any tangible link between Parnell and serious crime. The turning-point of the commission came in February 1889, when Richard Pigott's forgeries were dramatically uncovered under cross-examination by Parnell's counsel.

Marriage to Mary Yore

On 30 December 1886, while he was in the U.S., Davitt and Mary Yore had married, and she had returned with him to Ireland. Until his marriage Davitt did not have a home; being often on the move he had lived in hotels and boarding houses. On their marriage, the couple were presented with Ballybrack Cottage, the only token of esteem from his admirers that Davitt ever accepted. Wilfrid Scawen Blunt, who visited them the following summer, described it as 'a little bit of a cottage with an acre of ground, and the most lovely view in the world'.[38] 'Mrs Davitt,' he added,

> is a nice little woman unmistakably Irish and unmistakably American. She seems very happy. Davitt explained that she did not understand politics yet, having been brought up in a convent and lived very quietly. She was rather shy in playing her part of hostess, but was helped by Davitt's sister, an older woman, and our luncheon was a very good one, much better than at the Archbishop's palace yesterday.[39]

On Blunt's first meeting with Davitt, in March 1886, he had found him 'an odd-looking man, dark, sallow, gaunt, disfigured by the loss of his right arm, which is gone from the shoulder'. Nonetheless, he held him to be 'a most superior man, with more of the true patriot about him than any of those I have yet met'.[40] They struck up an immediate friendship.

Another friend, Sophie O'Brien, recalled that his marriage to Mary helped Davitt to dispel some of the gloom and sharp spurts of temper to which he had been prone: 'She cured him of his depression by laughing at it.'[41]

Davitt and the Labour Movement

In the years following the abandonment of the land struggle Davitt became deeply involved in the British and Irish labour movements, which were to occupy an important place for the rest of his life. He saw the struggles of British and Irish labour and the movement for Irish independence as intrinsically linked, and came to believe that Irish independence could only be won with the support of the British working class.[42] While it was true that British workers often shared the attitudes of the government towards the Land League and Home Rule struggles, they did not, Davitt believed, bear the responsibility for Britain's treatment of Ireland. He also saw the interests of urban and rural workers as complementary, rather than opposed, a theme later to be taken up by James Connolly in *The Reconquest of Ireland*[43] and his successors on the left.

This was a formative point in the development of the British labour movement. The period between 1880 and 1893, a time in which Ireland became the predominant issue in British politics, also saw a socialist revival in Britain. The two were not unconnected, as it was around opposition to government policies in Ireland that several of the British radical and socialist organisations were to emerge. Moreover, the extension of the franchise in 1884 had important implications for both the Irish and the labour questions. For a time both the leaders of the labour movement and most of the Irish leadership were to place their main hopes in some form of co-operation with the Liberal Party.

For much of the 1880s and 1890s Davitt was based in London and was more involved in the British labour movement than in the Irish one, to the chagrin of some of his Irish followers.[44] However, he did remain in close contact with Irish developments. His high standing among British workers is reflected in the fact that he was invited to run as a workingmen's candidate in Sheffield in 1885, an offer that he declined, asserting that he could do more service for Ireland and for workers outside parliament.[45] In 1889 he acted as mediator in a bitter dock strike in Liverpool.[46]

In *Leaves from a Prison Diary* Davitt had expressed the hope that the constituencies might return 'a Labour Party fifty or sixty strong to the House of Commons, instructed to act independently of political parties and with a view to the interests of labour'.[47] Thus it was that he supported Keir Hardie's Independent Labour candidacy in the Mid-Lanark by-election in 1888, despite the fact that the Irish Parliamentary Party supported his Liberal rival. However, Gladstone's conversion to Home Rule in 1886, and the difficulties he faced in his efforts to promote it in the years that followed, led Davitt not only to favour Irish co-operation with the Liberals, but also to fear the impact of Labour candidates on Liberal constituencies.

The most downtrodden sector of the Irish workforce in the late nineteenth century was the agricultural labourers. Despite expressions of solidarity with them during the land war of 1879–81, and the fact that they had taken part in the conflict with landlords, they had gained very little from the struggle.[48] Parnell made efforts to improve the situation by introducing legislation favourable to labourers; but with tenant farmers in the ascendant, the interests of their employees were often overlooked. One organisation that campaigned on behalf of labourers was the Irish Democratic Trade and Labour Federation, led by P. J. Neilan, John O'Shea, John D. O'Shea and David Sheehan. Davitt was involved in setting up the Federation, and he presided over its formation at a convention in Cork on 21 January 1890. This was primarily an organisation of agricultural labourers and workers based in country towns. It was centred around Cork, in an area where the National Agricultural Labourers' Union had been strong in the 1870s.[49]

Davitt's support of the Irish Democratic Trade and Labour Federation elicited a hostile response from Parnell, who questioned the need for a labourers' organisation.[50] The Federation was short-lived, however, and was to be swept away in the wake of the Parnell split. Nevertheless, in 1894 a new body, the Irish Land and Labour Association, arose to replace it. Once again, as its leader, D. D. Sheehan, relates in his memoirs, while Davitt welcomed it as being democratic and progressive, there was intense opposition mounted against it by other nationalist leaders.[51] Representing different strands of the parliamentary movement, John Redmond, John Dillon and William O'Brien viewed a specifically labour organisation as a divisive force in nationalist politics, although they courted its members' support

and the United Irish League attempted to bring it under its
influence. Nevertheless, the Land and Labour Association
managed to steer a more or less independent course and
continued in existence into the 1920s and even in small pockets
of the country into the 1930s.

Given Davitt's concern for the interests of labour, he tried to
induce the Irish Parliamentary Party to take a more active stance
in support of trade unions and the labour movement. He had
little success, however. In late 1890 he suggested to John Martin,
the president, and John Simmons, the secretary of the Dublin
Trades Council, that a conference of trade unionists should be
held in Dublin to discuss the formation of a general labour federation for Ireland. This met in 1891 and led to the foundation,
three years later, of the Irish Trade Union Congress. Davitt's
suggestion is likely to have been prompted by a wish to see the
Irish trade unions able to exert an influence on the Irish Party
similar to that which the British T.U.C. had on the Liberal Party in
areas of social reform.[52] This did not materialise, however,
perhaps owing to the fact that industrial workers occupied a much
smaller proportion of the population in Ireland than in Britain,
and would have tended to support the Irish Parliamentary Party
in any case.

From time to time Davitt was called upon to act as an arbitrator in industrial disputes, as, for example, in that between the
Dublin United Builders' Labourers' Trade Union and their
employers in March 1890.[53] On other occasions he spoke out in
support of workers' organisations, as when the workers of the
Great Southern and Western Railways came out on strike against
dismissals in April 1890.[54] In 1904 he defended the Dublin and
District Tramwaymen's Union in its claims against William
Martin Murphy's company, which refused to recognise the
union or its demands.[55] While welcoming the new unionism, he
opposed the incursions of British unions into Ireland, holding it
to be important that Irish workers have their own separate struc-
tures.

One of Davitt's initiatives which was aimed to benefit both
British and Irish workers was the launch of a penny weekly
newspaper, the *Labour World*, in September 1890. Since the late
1870s he had cherished the idea of editing his own paper.[56] The

new weekly was published in London and was at first successful; some 60,000 copies of the second issue were ordered. A substantial paper of sixteen pages, it provided a wide range of subject-matter, including foreign news, labour news from Britain, Ireland and America, notices of meetings, features, general political news, racing tips, short stories and poetry, a letters page, book reviews and a women's column. Among the issues it addressed were the plight of agricultural labourers in England, Ireland and Scotland; women in the workplace, including an article which advocated the employment of female factory inspectors; the work of the Salvation Army; discussion of the Fabian Society; land reform in Australia; the new unionism; and the ownership of capital. In tone it was more socialist than liberal. Unfortunately the paper was dogged by difficulties. Davitt's health broke down after four months, there were problems with printers, and eventually funding for the paper proved insufficient, and Davitt himself was taken up with campaigning over the Parnell leadership issue. The paper ceased printing in May 1891.[57]

The O'Shea Divorce

However, it was in the pages of the *Labour World* that Davitt published his call to Parnell to resign his leadership of the Irish Parliamentary Party in the wake of the divorce court finding against him. It is hard to credit that Davitt was completely unaware of Parnell's relationship with Katharine O'Shea. Prominent figures within the Irish Parliamentary Party had known of it since February 1881, when a letter addressed to Parnell was opened in Paris after he failed to keep an appointment with them.[58] The Liberal government came to hear about it in the course of that year.[59] There had even been some hints concerning it in the press, particularly during the Galway election campaign in 1886, when Parnell had foisted Captain O'Shea on the constituency.[60]

Nevertheless, in December 1889, when O'Shea initiated proceedings for divorce against his wife, naming Parnell as co-respondent, there was a tendency among Irish leaders to see this as yet another politically motivated attack, similar to the 'Parnellism and Crime' charges, and to hope that it would blow over. Davitt recalled that his associates hesitated to broach the subject with Parnell, but that when he did so, he received assurances that 'there was no peril of any kind to him or to the movement in Captain O'Shea's "threatened proceedings"' and that 'he would emerge from the whole trouble without a stain on his name or reputation'.[61] Davitt appears to have misunderstood these assurances to suggest that there was no liaison, whereas Parnell may have intended them to mean that there had been no dishonourable conduct. Davitt repeated what he believed to be the truth to English Home Rulers, telling W. T. Stead that Parnell 'has never deceived me in his life'.[62]

Davitt therefore felt betrayed when the truth came out, fuelling his resentment against his once-trusted leader. It was not this alone, however, which led him to be the first to call publicly for Parnell's resignation as leader of the party until he could marry Katharine O'Shea. For Davitt, the cause was more important than the individual, and he understood the damage the issue could do to the Liberal alliance. 'In this, the supreme crisis of his career,' he wrote, 'every true friend of Home Rule, every right-minded man in the three countries, will expect Mr Parnell to perform this act of self-denial in the best interests of the Irish people and their cause.'[63] There was also, undoubtedly, a degree of pent-up irritation at Parnell's frequent absences over the past years, coupled with the personality cult that had built up around him.

The Parnell Split

Davitt's opposition to Parnell's continued leadership of the Irish Party aligned him with the clerical and right-wing voices in Irish public life, men such as Timothy Healy and John Barry, with whom he had otherwise little in common. Nevertheless, he took a central part in the opposition to Parnell, organising the victorious North Kilkenny by-election campaign with Healy, despite his distaste for the candidate, Sir John Pope-Hennessy, 'that tricky politician'.[64]

The tone of exchanges soon became embittered, with Parnell accusing Davitt of disloyalty and Davitt replying with allegations of dictatorship and sneers at Parnell's aristocratic background. At a meeting in Ballinakill during the North Kilkenny election he replied to an attack by Parnell: 'If he was miserable scum he had the honour of being a poor evicted peasant's child, and not the descendent of a common Cromwellian soldier.'[65] During the North Sligo election in April 1891 Parnell asked his audience if they could follow 'a hysterical Davitt, who never belongs to any party for twenty-four hours together'. Davitt's response challenged his former leader's new-found radicalism, mocking his call for an eight-hour working day with his own addition to the rash of scurrilous rhymes that accompanied the Parnell split:

> Eight hours work and eight hours play,
> Eight hours in company of Mrs O'Shea.[66]

In an ironic twist of events, Davitt, the former Fenian, condemned Parnell's appeal to the 'hillside men' and to Fenian opinion in the country, claiming that it would be 'a piece of criminal folly for him or any other man to ask the young men of Ireland to face the overwhelming might of England in the field', and asserting that Parnell was only making the appeal in the hope of reaping political gains from it.[67] This is a further signal of how far Davitt had now moved away from the militancy of his youth.

On 10 March 1891, following the split in the Irish Parliamentary Party, the anti-Parnellite section left the National League and established the National Federation, of which Davitt was appointed secretary. The structure of the new body replicated its parent organisation, and all the council members except Davitt were members of parliament. Its establishment was another indication of the depth of the divisions in the national movement.

Following the North Sligo election, Davitt departed for America and remained there until early in 1892. Parnell died on 6 October 1891, marking a tragic end to an era that had promised so much for national hopes. Davitt's later writings about him display an impressive balance between criticism of his faults and appreciation of his achievements; and despite all that had happened, he continued to admire him as a great leader.[68]

4

THE PARLIAMENTARIAN, 1891–9

In the early 1890s, as a result of the split in the Irish Parliamentary Party and the death of Parnell, Irish nationalism was in severe crisis, divided into two warring camps, with the anti-Parnellite side further weakened by its own internal rivalries. F. S. L. Lyons described Home Rulers in 1892 as 'disunited, ill-disciplined, and with no outstanding leader, the very antithesis of the party which had assumed a role of such importance in 1886'.[1] The one remaining hope was with Gladstone, the ageing Liberal leader, whose commitment to Home Rule remained strong.

Until now Davitt had refused to stand for parliament, arguing that he could serve the national cause as well outside as inside the House of Commons and criticising an overemphasis on Westminster as the only means of achieving reform. While serving his term in Portland prison in 1882, he had been returned as M.P. for Meath. His election was a public act of solidarity with Davitt and defiance of the government on the part of voters. However, as a convicted felon, he was ineligible to take his seat.

In notes made in prison in 1881–2 Davitt assessed the main figures in the Home Rule Party, as part of a detailed analysis of the political situation of the time. Many, though not all, of his comments on individual Home Rulers were critical: Edmund Dwyer Gray—'able, adroit and ambitious'; T. P. O'Connor—'able, ambitious, needs care; [holds] English radical more than Irish national opinions'; F. H. O'Donnell—'a most accomplished fraud, dishonest, treacherous, and aiming for office'; W. H. O'Sullivan—'weak, but afraid to go wrong'; John O'Connor Power—'renegade to former nationalist principles: unscrupulously ambitious and untrustworthy'; T. M. Healy—'earnestness run riot; honest without judgement or discretion'; John Dillon—'thoroughly honest and unselfish but wanting in habits of reflection and calculation; liable to make mistakes and regret them; slight overdose of sincerity'; and Parnell—'sans peur et sans reproche'.[2] His sympathy for Parnell may have been strengthened by his clear appreciation of the weaknesses of Home Rule's parliamentary support, and he was keen in the 1880s to have more radical Irish M.P.s elected.

By 1884 Davitt's prison sentence had expired and he was invited to stand as a workingmen's candidate in Sheffield in 1885, an offer he declined, asserting that he could serve Ireland and the workers' cause better from outside parliament. Early in 1888, when Parnell suggested he run for election, he saw this as motivated by a wish to muzzle his outspoken support for the British labour movement, and again declined.

In December 1891, however, with the party weakened and support drifting away, Davitt was persuaded to stand as an anti-Parnellite candidate for Waterford City against John Redmond, the leader of the Parnellite side. Despite a letter from Davitt appealing for a truce between the opposed nationalist sides and expressing the hope that Waterford would not be the scene of violence as intense as that which had marred the Cork by-election in November, it was a very bitter campaign in which Davitt suffered an injury.[3] Redmond won the seat, but Davitt tried again the following July in North Meath. Here the over-zealous support of Bishop Nulty and other clerics resulted in Davitt's election being overturned on petition, on the grounds of clerical interference. Davitt, who had invested in the campaign, had to declare bankruptcy. In this election, in pursuit of his aims of achieving more radical representation for Ireland, he had recommended seven men as labour-nationalist candidates for Irish constituencies, of whom two were returned. In 1893 he was at last elected for North-East Cork. The previous year had seen Gladstone returned to power, pledged to another attempt to enact Home Rule for Ireland. Davitt was more than ever committed to the Liberal alliance. He was also on close terms with John Morley, Liberal Chief Secretary for Ireland from 1892 to 1895.

Davitt's support for the Liberal alliance tended to set him in opposition to Keir Hardie, the founder of the Independent Labour Party, who was contesting seats against it.[4] Moreover, Davitt questioned Hardie's commitment to Home Rule for Ireland, while Hardie, on his side, deeply disapproved of Davitt's

stance against Parnell during the divorce crisis. After 1895,
however, with a shifting political situation, there was a gradual
rapprochement between the two men.[5]

Unlike Parnell, who was an enthusiastic and effective parliamentarian,[6] Davitt deeply disliked Westminster, which he referred
to as 'parliamentary penitentiary'. There may have been an
element of the old Fenian opposition to participation in parliament in this attitude, and Davitt knew that in agreeing to enter
the house he was distancing himself from earlier ties.
'Remember', he wrote to Dillon in 1898, 'I have all but alienated
almost all my American friends through entering the British parliament. What was a serious sin in others becomes a mortal one
when committed by yours truly.'[7] In addition, Davitt hated the
atmosphere of a gentlemen's club that prevailed at Westminster.
Nor were the 1890s a happy time to be an Irish M.P there, with
the party in the doldrums and riven by rivalries and animosities.
Nevertheless, Davitt became an influential figure among Irish
M.P.s and was able to fulfil a useful role both for Ireland and for
the burgeoning labour movement.

Davitt was present in the House of Commons and participated
in the debates over the Second Home Rule Bill in 1893. In a long
maiden speech on 11 April he welcomed it as 'a pact of peace
between Ireland and the Empire, to be honourably upheld on
both sides' and described it as 'a compromise between absolute
independence, such as I once dreamt could be won for Ireland,
and government by force and unconstitutional means on the
other'.[8] From the beginning the bill faced fierce opposition.
Mauled in the committee stage, it was finally passed in the
Commons on 2 September, to be resoundingly defeated in the
House of Lords seven days later.[9] Gladstone retired in the
following March, and his successors as Liberal leader were eager
to distance themselves from Home Rule. Its prospect receded,
therefore, for nearly two more decades.

In 1895 Davitt undertook a seven-month lecture tour through
Australia, Tasmania and New Zealand. This journey resulted in his
second book, *Life and Progress in Australasia*, in which he aimed to
introduce what were then seven separate colonies to an English
and Irish public.[10] With their large Irish populations, they had
provided considerable funds to support the land and Home Rule

struggles, and Davitt addressed some seventy-two public meetings during his visit.

Davitt left for Australia early in the year. On reaching Colombo he received the tragic news that his seven-year-old daughter, Kathleen, had died after a short illness. His first impulse was to return to Ireland, but his wife persuaded him to carry on with the trip as planned.[11]

Always an enthusiastic traveller, Davitt wrote a detailed and lively account of what he found. He received a warm welcome, particularly from the Irish settlers, and wrote of the various people he encountered, including Mark Twain, whom he met on a ship from Australia to New Zealand. The book provides vivid descriptions of the very varied landscape. But what he was most concerned with was the people, their lives and work, and how they governed themselves. As an author, Davitt provides more than description; his book is enlivened by his own opinions and reactions to what he found.

The Australasian colonies had been granted their autonomy shortly before Davitt's visit, and they now existed as separate self-governing colonies. While deploring the fact that Western Australia, with a population of some 45,000, had been granted its own parliament in 1890, whereas Ireland, with some five million inhabitants, had been denied it in 1886,[12] he was curious to examine the political systems and legislatures of each colony he stayed in.

Australia was at this time a leading source of gold, and Davitt was interested to tour the goldfields and interview the miners. He criticised the great disparities between the fortunes made by some of the mine-owners and the miserable wages received by miners, the poverty and underdevelopment of the mining towns and, in some instances, the lack of attention to miners' safety.

In one chapter Davitt discussed the mistreatment of the Australian Aborigines by white settlers;[13] in another he investigated the conditions of the Kanakas, South Sea islanders imported to work the sugar plantations under virtually slave conditions, visiting and interviewing the islanders in their settlements.[14]

The abundance of land provided opportunities for experiments in communal farming to settle the urban unemployed on the land and a number of these had been established along the

Murray River in South Australia. Davitt, who was very interested in these semi-socialist communities as a model for addressing the problems of the urban poor, visited several of them, recounting their strengths and weaknesses and describing the difficulties and opportunities they faced.[15] He also examined the growth of Labour parties in various parts of Australia and the reforming legislation they introduced when in power. It is likely that his observation of these parties was among the influences that encouraged his eventual move from the Liberal camp to support for the British Labour Party.

Davitt had praise for the contribution of the Catholic religious orders in the development of Australian education, and, perhaps surprisingly for one who was later to become engaged in heated controversy with the Irish clergy over denominational education, he defended the place of religion in state schools.[16]

Having been so closely involved in land reform issues in Ireland, Davitt was naturally anxious to examine land tenure and land legislation in Australia. His continuing support for the goal of land nationalisation is evident,[17] and he deplored the ownership by individuals of vast tracts of land, particularly where they were used for sheep or cattle grazing rather than tillage. Shipping of refrigerated meat from Australia to Europe was only beginning, but Davitt could foresee the dramatic implications it would have for European meat producers.

Something of a specialist on prisons, Davitt conscientiously toured all the examples he could find in Australia, Tasmania and New Zealand, even nominating St Helena in Moreton Bay, Queensland, as his choice 'whenever my fifth imprisonment comes along for opposition to England's anti-Home Rule government'.[18]

Davitt returned home to a changed political atmosphere. He had been returned to represent South Mayo in 1895 in a general election that brought the Conservative Party back to government. The combined nationalist vote had fallen, and Home Rule appeared unattainable in the foreseeable future. The Conservative victory had been expected to herald a return to the policies of coercion, but instead these years marked the appearance of what became known as 'constructive Unionism'. These were the policies aimed at ameliorating social and economic problems in Ireland, though whether or to what extent they were in fact aimed at undermining the demand for Home Rule is a moot point.[19] In 1894 Horace Plunkett founded the Irish Agricultural Organisation Society as a central co-ordinating body for the co-operative movement. In the following year he called together the Recess Committee, to which he invited representatives from all the political parties to press for the establishment of a Department of Agriculture and Industries for Ireland. In 1896 the Childers Commission, which had been set up to investigate the financial relations between Britain and Ireland, reported that for many years Ireland had been overtaxed as a result of the Union. A nationwide movement began to revise fiscal relations between the two countries, the anti-Parnellites agreeing, somewhat reluctantly, to participate in an all-party conference to protest against the situation and to seek redress. Davitt and Dillon remained consistently hostile to overtures from moderate reformers like Plunkett, as they saw them as designed to distract attention from the main issue of Home Rule.[20]

Dillon, who became leader of the anti-Parnellite faction after the resignation of Justin McCarthy on 3 February 1896, sought to impose tighter discipline over what had become a rather lax and demoralised party. In this he was opposed by Timothy Healy, who favoured a more devolved structure and who pursued a bitter rivalry against Dillon and his supporters until his eventual expulsion in 1900. Davitt worked closely with Dillon in these years and seconded his attempts to impose party discipline.[21] Discipline, however, was not enough to reinvigorate the party, nor to provide it with a sense of purpose in parliament or among its supporters. Even the Irish Race Convention, meeting in Dublin in September 1896, which aimed to gather representatives of the Irish diaspora to a celebration of their achievements and to use this as a spur toward reunification, had failed to bring about a rapprochement within the Irish Party. Despite much rhetoric about unity at the convention, neither Redmond nor Healy attended its proceedings.

Some of the nationalist leadership became disillusioned with parliamentary politics in these years and either returned to private life or looked to a revival of popular agitation. Preeminent among the latter was William O'Brien, who had been living in Mayo since the early 1890s. There he became aware of the difficulties facing the smaller farmers, and their unequal competition with the larger graziers for access to land. In 1897 he was the moving spirit behind a project undertaken by the Congested Districts Board to move ninety-five families to Clare Island, but he realised that such piecemeal measures were insufficient to address a larger problem. In January 1898 O'Brien launched the United Irish League, named in reference to the United Irishmen, the centenary of the 1798 rising being celebrated that year. The new movement was lent further urgency by the re-emergence of food shortage in the west in the winter of 1897, a fact to which Davitt drew attention in parliament.[22] Initially the League focused on a call for the breaking up of grazier holdings and the redistribution of the land among smaller farmers.

At first the parliamentary leaders were suspicious of the new movement, seeing in it only a diversion from what they viewed as the more important struggle for Home Rule.[23] However, Davitt soon threw himself enthusiastically into the campaign for better conditions for small farmers in the west. Indeed, as Paul Bew has pointed out, he was the only Irish leader of national importance who took part in the early stages of this struggle.[24] Dillon, to O'Brien's surprise, held aloof from the new organisation, preferring to concentrate on parliamentary politics, although Davitt tried to influence him to support it.[25] In some respects the United Irish League was a reincarnation of the Land League, and Davitt was able to reactivate some of the old Fenian network which had played a part in the earlier movement.[26] As it spread rapidly in 1898 and 1899, he was also in a position to put the U.I.L.'s case in parliament. It is not hard, therefore, to understand William O'Brien's sense of loss, still evident eleven years later in his memoir, *An Olive Branch in Ireland*, at Davitt's decision in October 1899 to resign his parliamentary seat, give up his Irish commitments, and travel to South Africa.[27]

Davitt and the Boer War

Irish interest in the struggle waged by the Boers against the British government went back to 1877, when a group of seven Irish M.P.s opposed the passage of the South African Confederation Bill. This initial expression of sympathy with the Boer cause was followed by the opening of negotiations between some of the Irish M.P.s and the Transvaal Committee in Amsterdam, which took place in 1880. The First Anglo-Boer War, which began in December 1880, lent a further urgency to the developing crisis over land in Ireland, in that the government was now engaged on two fronts. Gladstone first concluded an agreement over the Transvaal government early in 1881, before turning his attention to the introduction of his Second Land Act.

The Second Anglo-Boer War stirred Irish public opinion to a greater degree than the First. The Jameson Raid, which took place in later 1895, came at a time when morale in Irish political circles was particularly low. The Irish Parliamentary Party was still divided, following the Parnell split, into three warring factions, from which many former supporters now turned in disgust. The chances for Home Rule appeared very remote, and the achievements of constructive Unionism seemed to add, if anything, to nationalist demoralisation. In this context, support for the Boers in their struggle offered an issue around which Irish of different shades of nationalist opinion could rally. Among these, from the beginning, was Michael Davitt.

After a period of gradually worsening Anglo-Boer relations, the war broke out on 11 October 1899. In Dublin ten days earlier a meeting in Beresford Place, attended by some 20,000 people, had been addressed by Davitt, Maud Gonne, Arthur Griffith, T. D. Sullivan, W. B. Yeats and others. A Transvaal Committee was formed, which included James Connolly, Maud Gonne, Arthur Griffith, John O'Leary and Davitt, with the object of raising awareness of, and opposition to, the war. Either on its own or in co-operation with other sympathetic organisations, it held meetings around the country. Among these was a gathering at Aughanmore in County Mayo, hosted by the newly formed United Irish League, at which a proposal by Davitt was adopted, which read:

> That we cannot refrain from an expression of our approval of the conduct of some thousand of the British mules in the neighbourhood of Ladysmith in Natal, nor the expression of sincere hope that some fitting testimonial will be made to the common sense of these intelligent animals in following the example of British soldiers in running into the camp of the victorious Boers.[28]

The declaration of war was bitterly attacked in the House of Commons by Davitt. On 17 October he made a long and powerful speech in which he rebutted charges of treachery to the Empire in his support of the Boers and proposing as his own epitaph:

> Here lies a man who from his cradle to his grave was considered by his foes to be a traitor to alien rule and oppression in Ireland and in every land outside her shores.[29]

Nine days later he startled Irish public opinion by resigning his parliamentary seat 'as a personal and political protest against a war which I believed to be the greatest infamy of the nineteenth century'.[30] This was during a debate on a Supplementary Army Estimates Bill, in which he and other Irish M.P.s attacked the fact that Ireland had to contribute £10 million to a war she opposed, asserting that he would not 'purchase liberty for Ireland at the base price of voting against liberty in South Africa'.[31]

Feelings were already running high in Ireland when it was announced that the Colonial Secretary, Joseph Chamberlain, would receive an honorary doctorate from Trinity College, Dublin. On Davitt's suggestion, demonstrations were planned to protest against the award. Dublin Castle responded by banning the meeting, but amid pitched battles between police and demonstrators, gatherings occurred, addressed by members of the Transvaal Committee, amongst whom a rather shaken Davitt urged that no attempt should be made to injure Chamberlain physically.

Davitt was involved in an attempt to bring about European intervention in the war on behalf of the Boers, but this was frustrated, first by the hesitation of Colonel Villebois Mareuil, who was to have led the French contingent, and then by the colonel's death. Nevertheless, in February 1900, having secured a commission with Randolph Hearst's *New York American Journal*, to cover the war as a correspondent, Davitt sailed for Laurenço Marques on board the *Oxus*, arriving in Pretoria on 26 March, the day after his fifty-fourth birthday. He spent the next three months travelling around the two Boer republics, meeting the leaders, and visiting the First and Second Irish Transvaal Brigades.

It was only a matter of time before the small Boer army was defeated by the much greater resources of the British. As the army of General Roberts was advancing, Davitt decided to leave South Africa, after witnessing the last session of the Boer parliament, the Volksraad, before the British forces entered Pretoria. He returned to Ireland in July 1900, where he began to write his book, *The Boer Fight for Freedom*, published in New York and London in 1902. It carries a dedication to 'the memory of General Philip Botha, O.F.S. Army, who nobly died fighting for Boer independence against the arch-enemy of his race and country . . .'. For the late twentieth-century reader, it is perhaps the least attractive of Davitt's books. Davitt was keen to expose the hypocrisy of British policy in South Africa. But his attack on the Uitlander speculators shares some of the antisemitism that came to the fore during the war, as in his naming of individuals made rich by the mines, listing some forty-four Jewish names, referring to them sarcastically as '"Englishmen" and "Reformers" who, with Mr Cecil Rhodes have succeeded' in bringing about the war.[32] This is not to say that Davitt was as antisemitic as some of his contemporaries, and he was to play an honourable role in castigating attacks on Jews in other circumstances. It is rather that his dislike for wealth and privilege led him to share a common prejudice against Jewish wealth.

Davitt was deeply impressed by the calibre of the Boer fighters, and was stirred by the idea of a small nation standing up to the might of the British Empire. Nevertheless, it is striking that a man who had displayed such concern for the plight of the Australian Aborigines accepted without question the Boer account of their relations with the indigenous peoples of South Africa. He must have known of the Clan na Gael proposal to assist the Zulu king, Cetewayo, in his struggle against the British in the 1870s; yet when the enemies of the African peoples were the Boers and not the British, he was content to refer to them as 'kaffirs' and 'savages'.

The 1890s saw Davitt's range of activities widening, although his main commitments remained, as ever, Irish affairs and the labour movement. Participation at Westminster brought him into the centre of British and Irish political life. At the same time, he became more involved in international issues, seeking to link the Irish struggle for independence with those of other nations.

THE FINAL YEARS, 1900–1906

To view Davitt and his contemporaries only in the context of Irish affairs is to underestimate the range of their interests and influence. Alan O'Day has shown us the extent to which the participation of Irish M.P.s at Westminster extended into the international sphere.[1] Late nineteenth-century Britain was very consciously the centre of an empire and a leading—still, at least in popular perception, *the* leading—world power. A striking aspect of Davitt's thought is the extent to which he was conscious of Ireland's situation as one shared with other peoples within the British Empire, such as the Boers in South Africa and the movement for Indian self-government. As a nationalist he sympathised with contemporary national struggles; he had some contacts with Polish and Finnish nationalists; he met and was impressed by the Hungarian leader, Lojus Kossuth; and he supported the emergent Jewish nationalism in the form of Zionism. He was, moreover, deeply interested in international affairs in general, enjoyed travel, and at times in his career he worked as a foreign correspondent for American newspapers and for the *Melbourne Advocate*. Davitt's final years saw a continuation of his international contacts, coupled with a turning in British politics toward support of the emerging Labour Party, while in Ireland his commitment to land reform remained as strong as ever.

Davitt returned from South Africa to a newly and somewhat insecurely reunited Irish Parliamentary Party.[2] Despite their hopes of ending the split, this was not the resolution that the leaders of the United Irish League had wished. Since 1899 they had come to hope that the discredited parliamentary party would simply be eclipsed by a more vibrant United Irish League.[3] Davitt wrote in consternation to O'Brien, describing the projected unification as 'the Healy–Redmond snare'.[4]

Over the following two years the United Irish League continued to grow rapidly. In August 1901 the police estimated that the number of branches had risen to 989, with a total membership of nearly 100,000.[5] As the League expanded beyond its original base in the west, its programme altered from its original emphasis on attacking grazier farming to renewed opposition to landlordism, with rent strikes and calls for the introduction of compulsory land purchase.[6] This prompted the government to respond with coercion measures, which were introduced in early 1902. By September over half of the country and the city of Dublin had been proclaimed disturbed areas and brought under the provisions of the coercion act, while some forty prominent Leaguers were imprisoned.[7] Davitt, Dillon and O'Brien, by their support for the campaign, were once again courting arrest, although it is noteworthy that at this point George Wyndham's administration did not move against them. In the meantime, the parliamentary party's attitude toward the movement remained ambivalent. O'Brien was returned for parliament in 1900, but Davitt found him egocentric and difficult to work with, writing to Dillon that the gap between him and the 'Tsar' was 'too wide to be bridged over',[8] and the two men eventually quarrelled.

In autumn of 1902 Davitt and Dillon undertook a fund-raising tour of the U.S. Since the reunification of the party, financial support from America had revived. On 3 September, just before their departure, Captain John Shawe-Taylor published his invitation to representatives of the landlords and tenants to meet together in conference to attempt a satisfactory settlement of the land question. By the time they returned, the conference, chaired by Lord Dunraven, had already taken place, and in March 1903 the Chief Secretary, George Wyndham, introduced a land bill based on its recommendations. Davitt launched an attack on its provisions, both because of his continued support for a settlement based on land nationalisation and on the grounds that the terms offered to landlords were too generous (he had assailed the Ashbourne Land Act on similar grounds in 1885). He was joined in his opposition by Dillon and the *Freeman's Journal*. On 26 September 1903 he published a letter in the *Freeman* which described the Dunraven group as having achieved a 'counterrevolution' in the value of landed property which was 'without parallel in the history of agrarian or political reform'.[9]

Nor did Davitt see a settlement of the land question as a panacea for the ills of the countryside. He had long urged an increase in tillage at the expense of cattle farming, as a means of providing opportunities for more people to live on the land. In early 1906 an issue arose over the likelihood that the new Liberal government would allow the free importation of Canadian cattle, which would inevitably compete with Irish cattle production. Davitt was worried that calls for protectionist measures would align the Irish Party with the right in British politics. His radical-liberal background predisposed him to favour free trade rather than protectionism, a point on which he had clashed with Parnell in 1885.[10] Moreover, he felt that a call for protectionism was unrealistic and that the case for cheap food for the labouring masses in Britain was likely to prove irresistible. Rather, he looked for improvements in methods of 'growing cattle', such as those advocated by the Department of Agriculture and Technical Instruction, in which cattle would be fattened in Ireland, rather than shipped to England 'half finished'. He condemned Irish agricultural methods as 'slovenly' and 'wasteful',[11] and he noted that Irish agriculture was falling behind its European competitors. Davitt's criticisms were, as Paul Bew points out, an admission that the old Land League programme had run into major difficulties[12] and that something more than peasant proprietorship was needed.

Russia

Davitt visited Russia three times between 1903 and 1905. His first trip was as an investigator for the *New York American Journal* following a pogrom against the Jews in the town of Kishinev in the Russian province of Bessarabia. He had already shown an interest in Russian affairs. In November 1890 he had taken part in a mass meeting in London, held to protest against the persecution of Russian Jews, and he had acted as a revolutionary arbitrator in 1892 in a dispute between Russian and Polish socialists.[13]

The pogrom took place on 19 April 1903, commencing on Easter Sunday and continuing for two days, amid scenes of great brutality, looting, rape and mutilation. In all, 51 people were killed and at least 424 injured. Almost one-third of the buildings in the city were damaged or destroyed. As the news of what had happened began to filter out, Randolph Hearst, the millionaire owner of four American newspapers, including the *New York American*, established a relief fund and appointed Davitt to investigate the veracity of the reports and to examine causes and responsibilities.

Davitt reached Kishinev on 22 May and spent eleven days investigating the story, leaving from Warsaw on 31 May. On reaching Berlin, out of the range of Russian censors, he sent an impassioned telegram to the press, urging immediate assistance to the Kishinev victims.

Davitt's inquiry was important in several ways. When the news about what had happened reached Britain and the U.S., it was widely believed to be exaggerated. Davitt, by visiting the scene of the attacks, was able to verify the stories, which he investigated very thoroughly, comparing accounts of the events, seeking corroborating evidence where possible, and photographing sites and victims. On the whole, his findings tended to confirm many of the rumours, though not all, and he was able to refute the official Russian version of events and to show how the groundwork for the riots had been laid by an antisemitic paper, the *Bessarabets*.

Davitt's articles, first published in the *New York American*, were widely reprinted in other publications in Europe and America and quoted in public speeches in a wave of outrage against the atrocities. They were particularly influential because he was neither Jewish nor anti-Russian and was obviously trying to be as objective as possible. The articles were further useful in assisting attempts to provide material support to the victims.

Not content with covering the pogrom for the press, Davitt went on to publish a book about it, *Within the Pale: The True Story of Anti-Semitic Persecutions in Russia*.[14] Here he traced the background to the position of Jews in Russia and then went on to examine the 'blood libel', which was used as an incitement to this and many other pogroms. Terming it a 'murder-making legend', he called upon Tsar Nicholas II and the Minister of the Interior, Plehve (a notorious antisemite), to deny publicly that the Jews were guilty of ritual murder. He even included quotations from seven medieval papal bulls condemning the accusation. He went on to discuss the position of Jews in the Russian Empire at the time, concluding that it was hopeless and that the best thing for the Russian Jews would be to set up a Jewish state in Palestine. This was the same conclusion that Theodore Hertzl, the father of modern Zionism, had reached in his book, *Der Judenstaat* (1896). Finally, Davitt turned to the events in Kishinev, describing the city, the attacks, the victims and the attackers, whose identities were widely known, as well as discussing accusations of government connivance in planning and executing the pogrom. He blamed the event primarily on three factors: economic rivalry, Russian legislation which put the Jewish population outside the law, and the 'blood libel'.

He was to repeat his refutation of the blood libel a year later in Ireland, when in a letter to the *Freeman's Journal* he protested at the behaviour of Father Creagh, a Redemptorist priest who had stirred up attacks on Jews by his antisemitic sermons in Limerick.[15] In recognition of his sympathy towards them, the Jews of Ireland sent a wreath to Davitt's funeral in 1906.

Davitt visited Russia twice more, in 1904 and 1905, working as a foreign correspondent. His perception of the British Empire in these years was strongly influenced by the policy of the Irish-Americans. British neutrality in the Spanish-American War in 1898 and American benevolent neutrality towards Britain in the Boer War resulted in a growing atmosphere of friendliness between the governments of Britain and the United States, and there was some suggestion in the early years of the century that an Anglo-American treaty might result. This was strongly opposed by Irish-American opinion, expressed, for example, by Clan na Gael and the United Irish Societies, which argued that if such a treaty were to occur, it should not come before Irish independence. In 1897, when an Anglo-American arbitration treaty had been mooted, Davitt had been active in lobbying senators and ensuring its defeat. He renewed this activity in 1904, spending the early months of that year in America. The British consul-general in New York, Sir Percy Sanderson, later commented to the British ambassador, James Bryce, that 'There is no doubt in my mind that the Irish, helped on by Michael Davitt's presence, exerted a strong influence on Congress at the time that the . . . negotiations for an arbitration treaty were under way.'[16] When, strengthened by the Anglo-Japanese alliance of 1902, Japan went to war with Russia in 1904, the Irish in America were firmly behind the Russians, holding mass meetings at which Russian flags were flown. Since 1877, when the British favoured Turkey in the Russo-Turkish War, John Devoy and Clan na Gael had engaged in intermittent contacts with the Russian government. It is against this foreign policy background that Davitt's articles in the *Irish World*, accusing Japan of 'playing England's game' in the Far East, and his pro-Russian journalism on his visit to Russia in 1904–5 must be viewed.

In mid-April 1904 Davitt was asked by Hearst's newspapers to report on the situation in Russia, in response to news stories in the *London Standard* that the empire was weakened in its military ambitions by high levels of discontent among industrial workers, which meant that troops had to be maintained in the cities of European Russia. He arrived in St Petersburg on 5 June, travelled on to Moscow for four days and then returned to the capital, leaving on 30 June and proceeding via Helsinki to Stockholm. Armed with a letter of introduction from Count Cassini, the Russian ambassador in Washington, Davitt was able to interview the First Secretary of the Russian Foreign Office, N. G. Hartwig (1855–1914) within days of his arrival.[17] He also toured the industrial suburbs of St Petersburg and interviewed Russians 'outside the works, in the tea houses, on the streets and near the churches'. He expressed the conviction that there was no basis for the newspaper claims of Russian unrest, and that these were 'invented to do injury in European countries to Russian interests and are worthy, in every way, of English methods of fighting a nation she hates because she dreads'.[18]

Davitt's third visit to Russia was in response to 'Bloody Sunday', the shooting of unarmed demonstrators in St Petersburg on 22 January 1905. By the following day Davitt was in London, where he met with the *New York American*'s agent, Flynn, and by the night of 24 January he was in Ostend, *en route* for Russia. Further unrest was expected on the Sunday following the atrocity, although Davitt was assured in an interview on 28 January with General Trepov, Deputy Minister of the Interior and Chief of Police, that there would be no recurrence, and in fact none occurred.[19] Davitt even applied for an audience with the Tsar, but was politely informed that requests from foreigners to be received in audience with the emperor had to be made by the relevant embassy to the Russian Ministry of Foreign Affairs.[20] He also asked to be allowed to interview those journalists imprisoned in the Fortress of SS Peter and Paul for reporting the events of Bloody Sunday, in order to enable him to refute rumours that they had been ill-treated, but was refused.[21]

Davitt's conclusions concerning the events of early 1905 were that their extent had been exaggerated in the press, that there was no revolutionary situation, that the demands of the workers were purely economic and not political, and that the Russian peasants were firmly against revolution and saw the Tsar as their protector. We now know in hindsight that what happened in 1905 was far more serious for the regime than he perceived and that both workers and peasants were in fact making political as well as economic demands.

How is it that Davitt could have misread the situation to this extent? In the first place, he was deeply influenced by his conviction that the British government was carrying on a propaganda campaign against Russia. Secondly, he was in Russia at a time when the revolutionary movement was still very scattered and diffuse. In addition, he had not experienced a police state before, and he may have underestimated the barriers of language and class that would have militated against workers addressed casually on the street speaking openly to him. Ironically, when he received a translation of what may or may not have been a genuine revolutionary manifesto, urging Russians to 'Arm yourselves . . . Only by force and blood will you obtain freedom and justice', denouncing the war in Manchuria, urging workers to strike, and concluding with the exhortation 'Down with Tsar Assassin. Long live the popular Assembly', Davitt dismissed it with a note: 'Did not use this. Manifestly written for consumption [by] English correspondents.'[22]

Indeed, in an article in the *Chicago Citizen* on 25 February he compared Russian and Irish conditions, concluding that there 'does not seem to be any material difference between them'.[23]

Davitt's reports provoked a blistering attack in the *Oakland Tribune*, entitled 'How Are the Mighty Fallen'. It accused him of acting as an apologist for the atrocities of a despotic regime, asking: 'Where is the voice that thundered against British tyranny from an Irish prison? Where the agitator that stirred the very bogs of Ireland to revolt against Saxon rule?'[24]

Once can sense that Davitt was more comfortable in covering the nationality questions in Finland and Poland. On the day he arrived at Helsinki, 6 February 1905, the Chief Procurator, Soisalo-Soininen Johnsson, was assassinated as a protest against Russian suppression of Finnish political autonomy. Five days later Davitt was in Warsaw, where a small insurrection had taken place in the last days of January. Here strikes had been organised by the Polish socialist party and Jewish socialists of the Bund in protest at the events of Bloody Sunday. Demonstrations turned to rioting, martial law was declared, and the military fired into crowds, killing around one hundred people. Davitt spent three days in Warsaw before returning home to Ireland.

During Davitt's trips to Russia in 1904 and 1905 he made two visits to Yasnaya Polyana, to visit and interview Leo Tolstoy. Sharing as they did a passionate interest in social issues, particularly in prison reform[25] and questions of land tenure, an admiration for the writings of Henry George and a detestation of the Boer War, they quickly established a rapport. They differed, however, in that Tolstoy was at the time the world's leading pacifist thinker, whereas Davitt was prepared to countenance armed struggle in defence of national self-determination.

In May 1904 Davitt published the last and the best-known of his six books, *The Fall of Feudalism in Ireland, or The Story of the Land League Revolution.*[26] Over 700 pages long, it presented Davitt's account of the land struggle, from the New Departure to 1903, with a detailed historical introduction outlining Irish history from the time of Oliver Cromwell. Providing as it does an insider's view of events and Davitt's assessment of the personalities and issues involved, the book has remained an important source for an understanding of the period.

The Origins of the British Labour Party

Since 1895, with the Liberal Party's abandonment of Home Rule, Davitt had been moving closer politically to Kier Hardie's Independent Labour Party, while Hardie, for his part, sympathised with Davitt's stand against the Boer War. In 1905, with the formation of the Labour Representation Committee, Davitt threw his full support into winning labour representation in parliament, campaigning in the midlands, south Wales, Lancashire and Yorkshire. On 16 February 1906, three months before his death, he took part in the victory demonstration of the newly formed Labour Party in the Queen's Hall in London. The 1906 general election had seen a Liberal landslide in Britain, so large that any dependence on Irish votes was unlikely. In a newspaper interview on the election results, Davitt recognised that there would be no Home Rule Bill in the new parliament. By now he pinned his hopes on a Labour victory: 'When the Labour representation in the House of Commons is a hundred and fifty strong, as probably it will be in the very next Parliament, then we will talk about Home Rule. I am convinced that the balance of power will rest with the Labour Party in the next Parliament.'[27]

Denominational Education

Among the Irish leaders Davitt had always been the most outspoken critic of clerical interference in politics. His Fenianism had made him an object of clerical suspicion in the early years of the Land League, and in 1889 he had denounced the papal rescript about the Plan of Campaign. The last battle of his life was over denominational education. The controversy first emerged following the introduction by the Conservative government of the Education Bill of 1902, which endeavoured to create a national system of education that would at the same time safeguard the position of denominational schools. The Irish members of parliament were under pressure from the leaders of Catholic opinion, particularly from Cardinal Vaughan, to support Catholic schooling, and Dillon outlined the Irish Party's position in May.[28] Their stance on the measure deepened the rift between the Irish Party and the Nonconformist Liberals. Davitt, irritated by Dillon's efforts on behalf of the bill, and by a congratulatory resolution passed by the Irish Party on the occasion of the pope's jubilee, wrote angrily to him, deploring the sectarian trend of the party:

> I don't know where we are drifting, what with your own exertions for Vaughan and co., and the growing clerical treason against the national cause all over Ireland, and now

the making of the Irish 'national' party a Catholic party (for
that is how the resolution will be understood everywhere) it
begins to look as if we were drifting into a modern imitation
of the historic 'brass band'.[29]

On 15 January 1906, just before the general election, the
Bishop of Limerick, Edward O'Dwyer, published a letter in the
Freeman's Journal urging Irish support for the Conservative Party,
rather than for the Liberals, who were opposed to denominational education. Davitt responded in a long letter on 22 January,
defending state-aided, secular education with separate religious
education provided by the clergy of each denomination. This
touched off a bitter dispute in which Davitt was subjected to much
personal abuse, before the controversy was brought to a close
during Lent. Nevertheless, several Lenten pastorals, including
those of Bishop O'Dwyer and the Archbishop of Dublin, William
J. Walsh, contained veiled attacks on Davitt. A pamphlet on the
question which Davitt planned as a response was never
completed, owing to his death.

Davitt was still in the midst of a vigorous career when he died
at the relatively young age of sixty. Having had some teeth
extracted, he caught a cold and developed an inflammation of
the jaw, which turned to blood-poisoning. After a short illness he
died on 30 May 1906. His funeral service was at Clarendon Street
Church, the only one in Dublin that had been willing to receive
the body of the Fenian Charles Heapy McCarthy in 1878. He is
buried at his birthplace, in Straide, County Mayo. He was survived
by his wife Mary and his children, Michael, Eileen, Cahir and
Robert Emmet.

CONCLUSION

More than any other popular figure of his time, apart, perhaps, from Parnell, Davitt won the hearts of the Irish public during his lifetime and after. He was of the people, understood their struggles, and was fearless in their defence. William O'Brien, who fought several campaigns with him, claimed that

> What they understood and loved in Mr Davitt was not the philosopher—more often than not he spoke above the heads of his listeners—but the one-armed Fenian chief, the darling son of their own Mayo, evicted like themselves, saturated with a hatred of Landlordism as fierce as their own, returning untamed by penal servitude to the old struggle, by new methods, perhaps, but with the old, unconquered men gathering behind him. They followed him and worshipped the man, without comprehending, or indeed heeding, the theories, which, for the rest, whatever they might be, were sure to be generous and single-minded.[1]

Among those who knew him well he was greatly loved for his warmth and kindness, and his generosity to anyone in difficulty.[2] An example of this was when, early in 1901, on visiting James Stephens and finding him ill and destitute, he arranged that money due to himself should be paid to the 'Old Chief' on a monthly basis and anonymously.[3] He could at times be impatient and irascible and was given to bouts of self-doubt, but William O'Brien described him as 'one of the most captivating of companions, combining many of the charms of a child with those of one of the most masculine of men'.[4] O'Brien's wife, Sophie, described him as 'a very tender father and a very patient one'.[5] A prodigious worker and a prolific writer, he never made much money; his friends agreed that he was bad at managing it and observed that he tended to give it away readily to needy individuals and causes. His lecture tour to Australia in 1895 was undertaken to recoup the Davitt finances in the wake of his bankruptcy, but this did not stop him handing over £1,200, all the proceeds of his lectures in

Queensland, to the Irish Parliamentary Party election fund.[6] Fiercely independent, he would not accept financial assistance from his supporters and struggled financially for most of his life, until a legacy from his wife's aunt, Mary Canning, in 1904 enabled him and his family to live in comfort in Dalkey.

Davitt's achievement in his leadership of the Land League, specifically in managing to weld together the disparate social elements behind the movement, was a very remarkable one. Even if that coalition was ultimately to weaken in the grazier conflicts of the early twentieth century, it presented a sufficiently united front in the later decades of the nineteenth century to force fundamental change in favour of tenants on a government predominantly made up of substantial landowners.

Would the shift toward peasant proprietorship have come anyway, without a Land League? Probably yes, because it represented a profound social movement, a change in power relations between the rising Catholic middle class and a retreating Irish landlordism that had its roots far earlier in the nineteenth century. Nevertheless, the process was greatly sharpened and accelerated by the land war. Moreover, Davitt and his associates brought to the movement a focus and a radicalism that would not otherwise have been articulated so effectively.

So what the land war achieved was a peasant proprietorship that ultimately benefited the larger and middling tenants most. But does this mean that the smaller tenants and agricultural labourers were betrayed by the failure of the land movement to cater for their specific needs? In a sense they were. Irish agricultural labourers were poor and disadvantaged well into the twentieth century. The difficulties of small farmers remain an issue to the present day. It might be argued that one achievement of the land movement on behalf of the smaller farmers of the west was to force a Conservative government to abandon the traditional *laissez-faire* approach and set up the Congested Districts Board in 1891. This was a recognition that the problems of the west were so intractable that they called for drastic new measures in the form of the first development agency in these islands. Yet even this, despite extensive and sustained efforts by the C.D.B. and its successors, failed to overcome the structural problems facing disadvantaged small farmers.

Apart from the land question, the other dominant theme in Davitt's life was his opposition to British rule in Ireland. At times he liked to point to the distance between Britain's democratic traditions and its role as colonial ruler. Although on occasion he could sound anti-English, his dislike was mainly directed at the government rather than the people. Indeed, as the later part of his life shows, he did hope and work for closer co-operation between the labour movements of the two countries. While he was willing to campaign for Home Rule, his preferred goal for Ireland was the republican one of the Fenians. In contrast to many of his colleagues, Davitt's nationalism was more in the liberal pattern of the mid nineteenth century than its later development. His formative influences here were Davis and Mitchel, his nationalism non-sectarian and inclusive. It embraced cultural and economic spheres. Thus in 1884 he participated enthusiastically in the establishment of the Gaelic Athletic Association. A native Irish speaker, he welcomed measures to foster the language through the Gaelic League, and he was keen to have children learn Irish history. However, he lived at a time when nationalism in Europe was entering a deeply conservative phase, mirrored to some extent by the obscurantism and confessionalism of the Irish-Ireland movement. Davitt did not share this. Well-travelled and very widely read in European as well as Irish and English literature, he criticised the Irish-Ireland idea in two articles in *The Nationist* in February 1906, setting out his own vision:

> My idea of an Irish Ireland is an Ireland as politically independent as we can make it; with all her people well educated—in Gaelic, and in English, and in as many other languages as they wish to learn; cultivating every available acre of Irish soil, and exporting millions of what we can spare from our own needs to England, or to any other country, and receiving in economic exchange all the useful and needful articles we require . . . for it is often by importing required articles which a country does not manufacture that it learns how, in time, to make them.[7]

As a political thinker, Davitt is not easy to categorise. On occasion he referred to himself as a socialist. For example, in *Leaves from a Prison Diary* he advocated what he referred to as 'state socialism', which was close to the 'municipal socialism' advocated by the Fabians. In his memoir *The Land War in Ireland*

Wilfrid Scawen Blunt related that Davitt called himself a 'Christian socialist'.[8] At other times, however, he explicitly distanced himself from socialism. He was not a Marxist and was never a member of the First International, although a few Fenians, including John Devoy, were. He certainly encountered Marx's daughter, Jenny Marx-Aveling, and he knew Henry Hyndman, founder of the Social Democratic Federation and the first populariser of Marx's ideas in English. Perhaps Davitt might best be described in ideological terms as on the border between radical liberalism and socialism.

Nevertheless, despite the great respect in which he was held, even by those whose opinions would have differed profoundly from his own, Davitt's support for the labour movement in Britain and Ireland did serve to distance him from most of his nationalist colleagues. On the other hand, his support of the Irish Parliamentary Party may, as James Connolly contended, have alienated him to some degree from the Irish labour movement. Connolly, whose ideas in some respects resembled his own, and with whom he was acquainted since the pro-Boer campaign of 1899, tended to dismiss him as 'an unselfish idealist, who in his enthusiasm for a cause gave his name and his services freely at the beck and call of men who despised his ideals and would willingly, but for their need of him, have hung himself as high as Haman'.[9]

Although he was a loyal and self-disciplined supporter of the Irish Parliamentary Party, Davitt's ideas were always his own, and at times the opinions he expressed differed sharply from the mainstream of Irish middle-class nationalism. Had he sought to do so, he might have led a more radical breakaway group, but he made no such attempt, and he and a handful of those who thought like him remained within the broad movement. His political heritage remains, however, in a strain of rural radicalism that has persisted—never dominant but often present—in Irish politics to the present day.

It might be argued that whereas earlier critiques of the dominant discourse on Irish society and economy favoured amendments and improvements to the system, Davitt's aims encompassed far more thoroughgoing change that went considerably beyond the achievement of peasant proprietorship. In ways the originality of Davitt's thinking speaks to the Ireland of a century after him. In his principled turning away from Fenianism he was the first in a series of prominent Irish leaders to make the transition from the physical-force tradition to democratic politics. Yet his view of politics was never confined to parliamentary activity. He saw earlier than most the potential for local government and devoted much of his work to popular organisations—such as associations of the Irish in Britain—and to the labour movement. He took an important part in the early emergence of labour politics, and his newspaper, the *Labour World*, played a pioneering role in labour journalism.

Committed as he was both to the small farmers and farm labourers of rural Ireland and to the urban working class, Davitt sought to bring the two populations together in a struggle against privilege. Although doomed by the conditions of the time to failure, we can see in hindsight that his campaign for land nationalisation correctly foretold that private property in land would not prove a panacea for Ireland's agricultural or social ills. Rural depopulation continued, small farmers remained relatively disadvantaged, and no satisfactory means have yet been found to cope successfully with ecological problems facing the countryside.

More than most of his contemporaries, Davitt was sensitive to denominational issues and to the need to define Irish nationality in the inclusive traditions of the Young Irelanders. Moreover, he was sharply critical of clerical intervention in politics.

Davitt's role in initiating the first political organisation of Irish women, in the formation of the Ladies' Land League, should not be overlooked. At a time when the concept of separate spheres for men and women still held sway, with middle-class women expected to confine their attentions to the home and to philanthropic work, the Ladies' Land League broke new ground.

While he was above all an Irish nationalist, Davitt's critique of British rule nonetheless extended to the whole Empire and included sympathy with other subject nations, such as the Indians and Boers. His concern with the plight of minorities, whether of Jews or Maoris or Australian Aborigines, puts him ahead of his time.

It is thus, in the breadth of his vision as an Irish nationalist, social thinker and internationalist, that Davitt may fairly be seen as a founding father of Irish democracy.

NOTES

Introduction

[1] Paul Bew, 'Parnell and Davitt' in D. George Boyce and Alan O'Day (eds), *Parnell in Perspective* (London, 1991), pp 38–51.

[2] Samuel Clark, *Social Origins of the Irish Land War* (Princeton, 1979), ch. 8.

[3] T. W. Moody, *Davitt and Irish Revolution, 1846–82* (Oxford, 1981). My debt to Moody's work, particularly for Davitt's earlier years, is evident.

[4] See 'Select Bibliography'.

1

[1] 'Notes for Reminiscences' (TCD, Davitt Papers, MS 9344/459).

[2] Ibid.

[3] Davitt was to recall how the Irish community had to barricade their doors on Saturday nights to protect themselves from the local quarrymen (ibid., MS 9344/160). See also Moody, *Davitt,* p. 12.

[4] An informative source on Davitt's early years is John Dunleavy, *Michael Davitt and Haslingden* (Haslingden Local History Society, 1979).

[5] Francis Haran to Mary Davitt, 7 Nov. 1907, quoted in Moody, *Davitt,* p. 44.

[6] 'Notes for Reminscences' (TCD, Davitt Papers, MS 9344/459).

[7] For more detail on this incident see T. W. Moody, 'Michael Davitt and the "Pen" Letter', *Irish Historical Studies,* iv, no. 15 (Mar. 1945), p. 250; Moody, *Davitt,* pp 59–62.

[8] T. W. Moody, 'Michael Davitt in Penal Servitude, 1870–77', *Studies,* xxx, no. 120 (Dec. 1941), pp 517–30; xxxi, no. 121 (Mar. 1942), pp 16–30. For Davitt's own account see Michael Davitt, *The Prison Life of Michael Davitt, related by Himself, together with his Evidence before the House of Lords Commission on Convict Prison Life* (Dublin, 1882); and *Leaves from a Prison Diary, or Lectures to a 'Solitary' Audience* (2 vols, London, 1885; repr., 1 vol., Shannon, 1972).

[9] *Freeman's Journal,* 3 Sept. 1872; *Nation,* 7 Sept. 1872; *Irishman,* 7 Sept. 1872; *Universe,* 7 Sept. 1872; *Accrington Times,* 7 Sept. 1872.

[10] This willingness to use his new-found reputation for public political purposes might be taken as an indication of the direction Davitt's career would take. It contrasts with the path followed by Charles Kickham, who on his release from prison in 1869 deliberately rejected the chance of becoming a public personage, seeing it as incompatible with the principles of Fenianism as he understood them (as well as incompatible with his personality). See R. V. Comerford, *Charles J. Kickham (1828–82): A Study in Irish Nationalism and Literature* (Dublin, 1979), p. 101.

2

[1] Michael Davitt, *The 'Times'–Parnell Commission: Speech delivered by Michael Davitt in Defence of the Land League* (London, 1890), p. 2.

[2] These were John Patrick O'Brien, Charles Heapy McCarthy and Thomas Chambers. On 15 January McCarthy, his health undermined by ten years of imprisonment, collapsed and died, his funeral providing a further occasion for public demonstrations.

[3] John Devoy, 'Michael Davitt's Career', *Gaelic American*, pt 1, 3 Jan. 1906.

[4] *Irish World*, 13 Nov. 1880; quoted in Thomas N. Brown, *Irish-American Nationalism, 1870–1890* (Philadelphia & New York, 1966), p. 24.

[5] Moody, *Davitt*, p. 225.

[6] Michael Davitt, *The Fall of Feudalism in Ireland, or The Story of the Land League Revolution* (London & New York, 1904; repr., Shannon, 1970), p. 123.

[7] T. W. Moody, 'The New Departure in Irish Politics, 1878–9' in H. A. Cronne, T. W. Moody and D. B. Quinn (eds), *Essays in British and Irish History in honour of James Eadie Todd* (London, 1949) pp 303–33; Moody, *Davitt*, pp 122–3, 249–53, 261–5, 325–6.

[8] R. V. Comerford, *The Fenians in Context: Irish Politics and Society, 1848–82* (Dublin, 1985), p. 226.

[9] Davitt, *Fall of Feudalism*, p. 126.

[10] Marcus Bourke, *John O'Leary: A Study in Irish Separatism* (Tralee, 1967) p. 157.

[11] Paul Bew, *Land and the National Question in Ireland, 1858–82* (Dublin, 1978), pp 47–8.

[12] *Report of the Special Commission on Parnellism and Crime*, ix, 419 (3 July 1889); quoted in Moody, *Davitt*, p. 208.

[13] Lalor had influenced John Mitchel in his thinking on the land question, and Mitchel had brought these ideas with him to America, where he lived from the 1850s to the 1870s, making them known in Irish-American nationalist circles.

[14] The Irish response to these difficulties was echoed in rural parts of Britain, notably in the crofter movement in the Scottish Highlands and similar agitation among Welsh hill farmers. Eric Hobsbawm, *Industry and Empire*, Pelican Economic History of Britain, vol. 3 (London, 1968), p. 129.

[15] Moody, *Davitt*, p. 325; Moody, 'The New Departure in Irish Politics, 1878–9'.

[16] Moody, *Davitt*, p. 301.

[17] Devoy, 'Michael Davitt's Career', *Gaelic American*, pt 1, 3 Jan. 1906.

[18] *Montreal Evening Post*, 10 Mar. 1880; quoted in Moody, *Davitt*, p. 358.

[19] Patrick Lavelle, *The Irish Landlord since the Revolution* (Dublin, 1870); see also Gerard Moran, *A Radical Priest in Mayo: The Rise and Fall of Father Patrick Lavelle, 1825–86* (Dublin, 1994).

[20] Quoted in D. B. Cashman, *The Life of Michael Davitt, Founder of the National Land League* (London, 1882), p. 99.

[21] Bew, *Land and the National Question*, pp 61–2.

[22] For example, *Connaught Telegraph*, 11 Oct. 1879; quoted in Moody, *Davitt*, p. 322.

[23] *Report of the Special Commission on Parnellism and Crime, 1888* [Cd 5891], H.C. 1890, xxxvii Evidence of C. S. Parnell, 30 Apr. 1889, p. 37, paras 58608–17.

[24] Moody, *Davitt*, p. 381.

[25] Ibid., pp 379–80; Bew, *Land and the National Question*, p. 93; *Devoy's Post-Bag*, ed. William O'Brien and Desmond Ryan (2 vols, Dublin, 1948–53), i, 483, 495–6.

[26] Davitt, *Fall of Feudalism*, p. 112.

[27] Figures quoted from R. V. Comerford, 'The Politics of Distress, 1877–82' in W. E. Vaughan (ed.), *A New History of Ireland*, iv: *Ireland under the Union, I: 1801–70* (Oxford, 1989), p. 45; Moody, *Davitt*, Appendix E1, p. 565.

[28] This is explored in detail in Clark, *Social Origins of the Irish Land War*.

[29] William O'Brien, *Recollections* (New York & London, 1905), p. 205, identified four different meanings of the phrase.

[30] Clark, *Social Origins of the Irish Land War*, p. 255; Donald E. Jordan, jr, *Land and Popular Politics in Ireland: County Mayo from the Plantation to the Land War* (Cambridge, 1994), p. 190.

[31] This was the advice given by Malachy O'Sullivan at Westport. See Moody, *Davitt*, p. 321.

[32] Comerford, 'The Politics of Distress', pp 43–4.

[33] Anna Parnell, *The Tale of a Great Sham*, ed. Dana Hearne (Dublin, 1986); see also below, ch. 3.

[34] Bew, *Land and the National Question*, pp 142–3, 174–5.

[35] Ibid., p. 143.

[36] Davitt to Devoy, 16 Dec. 1880, *Devoy's Post-Bag*, ii, 21–5.

[37] In places class tensions between farmers and labourers came to the surface and checked the spread of the Land League. See Paul Bew and Frank Wright, 'The Agrarian Opposition in Ulster Politics, 1848–87' in Samuel Clark and James S. Donnelly, jr (eds), *Irish Peasants: Violence and Political Unrest, 1780–1914* (Manchester, 1983), pp 192–229.

[38] Paul Bew, 'Parnell and Davitt' in Boyce and O'Day (eds), *Parnell in Perspective*, p. 46.

[39] Davitt, *Fall of Feudalism*, p. 301; Clark, *Social Origins of the Irish Land War*, p. 292.

[40] Moody, *Davitt*, pp 368–9.

[41] Ibid., p. 439; Davitt, *Fall of Feudalism*, pp 298–9.

[42] Laurence J. Kettle (ed.), *The Material for Victory: The Memoirs of Andrew J. Kettle, Right-Hand Man to Charles S. Parnell* (Dublin, 1958), p. 39.

[43] Davitt, *Fall of Feudalism*, pp 301–2.

[44] Ibid., p. 299.

[45] Ibid.

[46] This was, in fact, Davitt's third sojourn in prison, as he had spent some time in Sligo jail in 1879.

[47] Michael Davitt, *Leaves from a Prison Diary, or Lectures to a 'Solitary' Audience* (2 vols, London, 1885; repr., 1 vol., Shannon, 1972).

[48] Davitt, *Fall of Feudalism*, p. 317.

[49] The clergy were, in fact, divided in their attitude to the Ladies' Land League; see Emmet Larkin, *The Roman Catholic Church and the Creation of the Modern Irish State, 1878–1886* (Dublin, 1976), pp 96–108. One American cleric, Bishop Gilmour of Cleveland, went so far as to declare members of the American branch of the Ladies' Land League excommunicate; see Brown, *Irish-American Nationalism*, p. 121; Davitt, *Fall of Feudalism*, p. 399.

[50] Janet K. TeBrake, 'Irish Peasant Women in Revolt: The Land League Years', *Irish Historical Studies*, xxvii, no. 109 (May 1992), pp 63–80.

[51] See ibid.

[52] There seem to have been several attempts coming from the local organisations to form women's branches of the Land League before the leadership's decision. See Moody, *Davitt*, p. 433.

[53] Toby Joyce, 'Ireland's Trained and Marshalled Manhood' in Margaret Kelleher and James H. Murphy (eds), *Gender Perspectives in Nineteenth-Century Ireland: Public and Private Spheres* (Dublin, 1997), pp 70–80.

[54] Quoted in Mary Cullen, 'Foreward' to Kelleher and Murphy (eds), *Gender Perspectives in Nineteenth-Century Ireland*, p. 7.

[55] Francis Sheehy-Skeffington, *Michael Davitt: Revolutionary, Agitator and Labour Leader* (London, 1908; repr., London, 1967), p. 217.

[56] There are several interesting studies of Anna Parnell and the Ladies' Land League. Among them are: T. W. Moody, 'Anna Parnell and the Land League', *Hermathena*, cxvii (summer 1974), pp 5–17; Dana Hearne, Introduction to Parnell, *Tale of a Great Sham*; Jane McL.Côté, *Fanny and Anna Parnell: Ireland's Patriot Sisters* (Dublin 1991); and Jane McL.Côté and Dana Hearne, 'Anna Parnell' in Mary Cullen and Maria Luddy (eds), *Women, Power and Consciousness in Nineteenth-Century Ireland* (Dublin, 1995).

[57] Michael Davitt, 'The Story of the Land War' [interview with *New York Daily World*] in Cashman, *Davitt*, p. 232.

[58] Davitt, *Fall of Feudalism*, p. 356.

[59] Philip Bull, *Land, Politics and Nationalism: A Study of the Irish Land Question* (Dublin, 1996), p. 100.

[60] Davitt, 'Story of the Land War' in Cashman, *Davitt*, p. 232.

[61] Davitt, *Fall of Feudalism*, p. 340.

[62] TCD, Davitt Papers, MS 9511/5599–604, quoted in Côté and Hearne, 'Anna Parnell', p. 278.

3

[1] Arrears of Rent (Ireland) Act, 1882 (45 & 46 Vict., c. 47), 18 Aug. 1882.

[2] Cashman, *Davitt*, p. 163.

[3] Davitt, *Leaves from a Prison Diary, or Lectures to a 'Solitary' Audience*, completed 1884, published, 2 vols, London, 1885; repr., 1 vol., Shannon, 1972.

[4] *Report of the Special Commission on Parnellism and Crime*, ix, 419 (3 July 1889); quoted in Moody, *Davitt*, p. 523.

[5] Fintan Lane, *The Origins of Modern Irish Socialism, 1881–1896* (Cork, 1997), p. 68.

[6] Henry George, *The Irish Land Question: What It Involves and How Alone It Can Be Settled: An Appeal to the Land Leagues* (New York & London, 1881), p. 21.

[7] Ibid.

[8] Ibid., p. 24.

[9] Ibid., p. 31.

[10] Michael Davitt, 'The Irish Social Problem', *To-Day*, no. 4, pp 241–55 (italics Davitt's).

[11] Davitt, *Leaves from a Prison Diary*, ii, 99.

[12] Ibid., p. 98.

[13] *United Ireland*, 2 Aug. 1885; quoted in Lane, *Origins of Modern Irish Socialism*, p. 88.

[14] C. E. H. Vincent to Harcourt, 11 May 1882, quoted in F. S. L. Lyons, *Charles Stewart Parnell* (London, 1977), p. 351.

[15] For the text of the proposal see Cashman, *Davitt*, pp 254–6.

[16] Davitt, *Fall of Feudalism*, p. 349.

[17] Alan O'Day, *Irish Home Rule, 1867–1921* (Manchester, 1998), pp 80–81.

[18] Davitt, *Fall of Feudalism*, pp 372–4.

[19] Ibid., p. 379.

[20] Ibid., p. 381.

[21] *Hansard 3 (Commons)*, cclxxxv, ii, 1766, (15 Mar. 1884); quoted in Mary Cumpston, 'Some Early Indian Nationalists and their Allies in the British Parliament, 1851–1906', *English Historical Review*, lxxvi (1961), pp 278–97.

[22] R. P. Masani, *Dadabhai Naoroji: the Grand Old Man of India* (London, 1939).

[23] Davitt, *Fall of Feudalism*, p. 447.

[24] Ibid.

[25] Cumpston, 'Some Early Indian Nationalists', p. 285.

[26] Moody, *Davitt*, p. 549. Alfred Webb later did so and served as President of the Congress for a year. (I am grateful to Dr Alan O'Day for this information.)

[27] Davitt's diary: interview with Kossuth, Turin, 24 Jan. 1885 (TCD, Davitt Papers, MS 9544).

[28] For example, *United Ireland* asserted that 'The Philosophical Radicals are merely rich bourgeois with a grudge against the aristocratic society from which their vulgarity excludes them' (*United Ireland*, 18 Feb 1882, editorial 'War on the Radicals'; quoted in Frank Callanan, *T. M. Healy* (Cork, 1996), p. 115).

[29] Walter L. Arnstein, *The Bradlaugh Case: A Study in Late Victorian Opinion and Politics* (Oxford, 1965), pp 205–7, 223; Callanan, *Healy*, pp 116–18.

[30] Davitt, *Fall of Feudalism*, p. 476. See also *Nation*, 4 July 1885; quoted in Alan O'Day, *Parnell and the First Home Rule Episode* (Dublin, 1986), p. 64.

[31] *Freeman's Journal*, 18 Aug.1885; quoted in O'Day, *Parnell and the First Home Rule Episode*, p. 81.

[32] William O'Brien, *Evening Memories* (Dublin & London, 1920), pp 157–8.

[33] This statement is contradicted by William O'Brien's account of a meeting with Parnell in the autumn of 1886 (*Evening Memories*, pp 155–7).

[34] Davitt, *Fall of Feudalism*, p. 519.

[35] *Irish Catholic*, 2 June 1888; quoted in Emmet Larkin, *The Roman Catholic Church and the Plan of Campaign in Ireland, 1886–1888* (Cork, 1978), p. 228.

[36] See Davitt, *Fall of Feudalism*, pp 549–60.

[37] Michael Davitt, *The 'Times'–Parnell Commission: Speech delivered by Michael Davitt in Defence of the Land League* (London, 1890).

[38] Wilfrid Scawen Blunt, *The Land War in Ireland: Being a Personal Narrative of Events* (London, 1912), p. 274.

[39] Ibid.

[40] Ibid. pp 50–51.

[41] Mrs William O'Brien, *My Irish Friends* (Paris, 1937), p. 32.

[42] On the other hand, Karl Marx believed that the British working class would never achieve anything before it had got rid of Ireland: 'The lever must be applied in Ireland' (E. Strauss, *Irish Nationalism and British Democracy* (London, 1951), p. 188).

[43] James Connolly, *The Reconquest of Ireland* (Dublin, 1920), pp 323–4.

[44] Lane, *Origins of Modern Irish Socialism*, p. 168.

[45] T. W. Moody, 'Michael Davitt and the British Labour Movement, 1882–1906', *Transactions of the Royal Historical Society*, 5th ser., iii (1953), pp 53–76.

[46] Ibid., p. 67.

[47] Davitt, *Leaves from a Prison Diary*, ii, 161.

[48] See J. S. Donnelly, jr, *The Land and the People of Nineteenth-Century Cork: The Rural Economy and the Land Question* (London, 1975), pp 234–42.

[49] P. L. R. Horn, 'The National Agricultural Labourers' Union in Ireland, 1873–9', *Irish Historical Studies*, xvii, no. 67 (Mar. 1971), pp 340–52.

[50] Davitt, *Fall of Feudalism*, p. 636.

[51] D. D. Sheehan, *Ireland since Parnell* (London, 1921), pp 174–84. See also Pádraig G. Lane, 'The Land and Labour Association, 1894–1914', *Journal of the Cork Historical and Archaeological Society*, xcviii (1993), pp 90–106.

[52] John W. Boyle, *The Irish Labor Movement in the Nineteenth Century* (Washington, D.C., 1988), p. 138.

[53] Lane, *Origins of Modern Irish Socialism*, p. 167.

[54] Boyle, *Irish Labor Movement*, p. 101.

[55] This was the same company which, in its dispute with Jim Larkin nine years later, was to spark off the 1913 lock-out.

[56] In 1889 he had been seen as a possible editor of the *Freeman's Journal*. See Larkin, *The Roman Catholic Church and the Plan of Campaign*, p. 191.

[57] Moody, 'Davitt and the British Labour Movement', p. 68.

[58] Davitt, *Fall of Feudalism*, p. 306.

[59] Conor Cruise O'Brien, *Parnell and His Party, 1880–90* (Oxford, 1957), pp 167–8.

[60] For example, *New York Times*, 26 Oct. 1888; see Callanan, *Healy*, p. 244.

[61] Davitt, *Fall of Feudalism*, p. 637.

[62] W. T. Stead, 'The Story of an Incident in the Home Rule Cause', *Review of Reviews*, ii (Dec. 1890), p. 600; see Callanan, *Healy*, p. 244.

[63] *Labour World*, 22 Nov. 1890, Editorial, 'Mr Parnell's Position'.

[64] Davitt to Richard McGhee, 12 Dec. 1890, quoted in Callanan, *Healy*, p. 393.

[65] *Freeman's Journal*, 17 Dec. 1890.

[66] *Sunday World*, 5 Apr. 1891.

[67] *Freeman's Journal*, 22 Dec. 1890; see also F. S. L. Lyons, *The Fall of Parnell, 1890–91* (London, 1960), pp 168–71.

[68] See especially Davitt, *Fall of Feudalism*, pp 651–9.

4

[1] F. S. L. Lyons, *The Irish Parliamentary Party, 1890–1910* (London, 1951), p. 38.

[2] Quoted in Moody, *Davitt*, pp 512–13.

[3] *Irish Times*, 14 Dec. 1891; Lyons, *Irish Parliamentary Party*, p. 33.

[4] The Independent Labour Party was founded in 1893.

[5] Moody, 'Davitt and the British Labour Movement', p.73.

[6] For an examination of this aspect of Parnell's career see Alan O'Day, *Charles Stewart Parnell* (Dundalk, 1998).

[7] Davitt to Dillon, 29 Oct. 1898, quoted in F. S. L. Lyons, *John Dillon: A Biography* (London, 1968), p. 182.

[8] *Hansard, 4 (Commons)*, xi, 44–5 (11 Apr. 1893).

[9] See O'Day, *Irish Home Rule*, pp 152–69, for a lucid and detailed account of events surrounding the Second Home Rule Bill.

[10] Michael Davitt, *Life and Progress in Australasia* (London, 1898).

[11] Mrs William O'Brien, *My Irish Friends*, p. 33.

[12] Davitt, *Life and Progress in Australasia*, p. 27.

[13] Ibid., ch. 8.

[14] Ibid., pp 269–80.

[15] Ibid., chs 17–19.

[16] Ibid., pp 126–7.

[17] Ibid., p. 296.

[18] Ibid., p. 423.

[19] For a discussion of this see Andrew Gailey, *Ireland and the Death of Kindness: The Experience of Constructive Unionism, 1890–1905* (Cork, 1987).

[20] Davitt saw the all-party conference as a dishonest movement designed to distract attention away from the main issues (Davitt to O'Brien, 1 Mar. 1897, quoted in Lyons, *Irish Parliamentary Party*, p. 69 n. 3).

[21] See, for example, his resolution of January 1897 providing for regular meetings of the parliamentary party, stating that it was contrary to the duty of any member to oppose publicly any decision reached by the party or its chairman; attacking the recently established People's Rights Fund started by Healy and urging that no member should associate with it; and adopting the sanction of expulsion for members who disregarded this warning (Lyons, *Irish Parliamentary Party*, p. 64).

[22] *Hansard, 4 (Commons)*, xlvii, 57 (5 Mar. 1897); ibid., 1024 (19 Mar. 1897).

[23] Davitt to O'Brien, 1 Mar. 1897, quoted in Lyons, *Irish Parliamentary Party*, p. 69 n. 3.

[24] Paul Bew, *Conflict and Conciliation in Ireland, 1890–1910: Parnellites and Radical Agrarians*, (Oxford, 1987), p. 39.

[25] For a fuller exploration of Dillon's approach to the U.I.L. see Lyons, *Dillon*, pp 181–5.

[26] Bull, *Land, Politics and Nationalism*, pp 135–6.

[27] William O'Brien, *An Olive Branch in Ireland and its History* (London, 1910), p. 107.

[28] PRO, CO 903/8, 'Irish Crimes Record, 1899', pp 5–6, 10, 12; quoted in D. P. McCracken, *The Irish Pro-Boers, 1877–1902* (Johannesburg, 1988), p. 56.

[29] *Hansard, 4 (Commons)* lxxvii, 129 (17 Oct. 1899).

[30] Michael Davitt, *The Boer Fight for Freedom* (New York & London, 1902), p. v.

[31] *Hansard, 4 (Commons)*, lxxvii, 614–22 (25 Oct. 1899).

[32] Davitt, *Boer Fight for Freedom*, p. 29.

5

[1] Alan O'Day, T*he English Face of Irish Nationalism: Parnellite Involvement in British Politics, 1880–86* (Dublin, 1977) ch. 10: 'Overseas Affairs and Parnellite Imperialism'.

[2] This accord was achieved at a meeting in the House of Commons on 30 January 1900.

[3] Philip Bull, 'The United Irish League and the Reunion of the Irish Parliamentary Party, 1898–1900', *Irish Historical Studies*, xxvi, no. 101 (May 1988), pp 51–78.

[4] Davitt to O'Brien, 23 Jan. 1900, quoted ibid., p. 68.

[5] Report by District Inspector E. V. W. Winder, 7 Aug. 1901 (N.A.I., Crime Branch Special Papers, 24995/S; quoted in Lyons, *Dillon*, p. 223).

[6] On the impact of the campaign for compulsory land purchase see Fergus Campbell, 'Land and Politics in Connacht, 1898–1909' (Ph.D. thesis, University of Bristol, 1996), ch. 3.

[7] O'Day, *Irish Home Rule*, p. 193.

[8] Davitt to Dillon, 22 Sept. 1900, quoted in Lyons, *Dillon*, p. 215.

[9] *Freeman's Journal*, 26 Sept. 1903; quoted in Bew, *Conflict and Conciliation*, pp 103–4.

[10] Davitt, *Fall of Feudalism*, pp 478–9.

[11] *Irish Independent*, 13 Mar. 1906; quoted in Bew, *Conflict and Conciliation*, p. 126.

[12] Bew, *Conflict and Conciliation*, p. 128.

[13] John Slatter, 'An Irishman at a Revolutionary Court of Honour: from the Michael Davitt Papers', *Irish Slavonic Studies*, no. 5 (1984), pp 33–42.

[14] Michael Davitt, *Within the Pale: The True Story of Anti-Semitic Persecutions in Russia* (New York & London, 1903; repr., New York, 1975).

[15] Louis Hyman, *The Jews of Ireland: from Earliest Times to the Year 1910* (Shannon, 1972), p. 212.

[16] Sanderson to Bryce, 23 Feb. 1907, in Bryce to Hardinge, 7 Mar. 1907 (PRO, FO 371/359; quoted in Alan J. Ward, *Ireland and Anglo-American Relations, 1899–1921* (London, 1969), p. 55).

[17] TCD, Davitt Papers, MSS 9507/5478, 5494. They met on 8 June 1904.

[18] Ibid., MS 9507/5493.

[19] Ibid., MS 9508/5538.

[20] Ibid., MS 9508/5496.

[21] Ibid., MS 9508/5530.

[22] Ibid., MS 9508/5499.

[23] Ibid., MS 9508/5529.

[24] *Oakland Tribune*, 7 Feb. 1905, Editorial.

[25] Davitt had read Tolstoy's novel *Resurrection*, which publicised the terrible conditions of the Siberian convict system.

[26] Michael Davitt, *The Fall of Feudalism in Ireland, or The Story of the Land League Revolution* (London & New York, 1904; repr., Shannon, 1970).

[27] *Irish People*, 10 Feb. 1906; quoted in Bew, *Conflict and Conciliation*, p. 124.

[28] *Hansard 4 (Commons)*, cvii, 997–1009 (17 May 1902).

[29] Davitt to Dillon, 1 Aug. 1902, quoted in Lyons, *Dillon*, p. 221.

Conclusion

[1] William O'Brien, *Recollections* (London, 1905), p. 269.

[2] These are too numerous to list here. Davitt's personality was also portrayed in a novel by Edna Lyall [Ada Ellen Bayly], entitled *Doreen* (1894), in the character of Donal Moore, although some of the details were altered. See also J. M. Escreet, *The Life of Edna Lyall* (London, 1904), pp 137–44, 148.

[3] TCD, Davitt Papers, MS 9659c/77/1.

[4] O'Brien, *Olive Branch*, p. 114.

[5] Mrs William O'Brien, *My Irish Friends*, p. 32.

[6] Davitt to James Collins, 19 Aug. 1895 (TCD, Davitt Papers, MS 9659c/45/1).

[7] *The Nationist*, 1 Feb. 1906; quoted in Sheehy-Skeffington, *Davitt*, p. 198.

[8] Blunt, *The Land War in Ireland*, p. 93.

[9] James Connolly, 'Michael Davitt: A Text for a Revolutionary Lecture' in *James Connolly: Selected Political Writings*, ed. Owen Dudley Edwards and Bernard Ransom (London, 1973), pp 210–15. This is a review of Francis Sheehy-Skeffington's biography of Davitt.

SELECT BIBLIOGRAPHY

Although in the early 1890s Davitt planned to write an autobiography (which he variously considered calling 'A Life's Labour
in Ireland', 'Memories of Strife', 'Revolutionary Recollections',
'The Autobiography of an Activist' or 'Forty Years of Conflict in
Ireland'), in the end he never succeeded in doing so. However,
each of the six books he published in his lifetime includes information about his life and thought.

Leaves from a Prison Diary, or Lectures to a 'Solitary' Audience (2
vols, London 1885; repr., 1 vol., Shannon, 1972) provides some
description of Davitt's first prison experience and an analysis of
prisons and their inmates in the first volume and ideas for social
reform in the second. It was largely written when he was serving
his second prison term in 1881–2.

*The 'Times'–Parnell Commission: Speech delivered by Michael Davitt
in Defence of the Land League* (London, 1890) is based on Davitt's
evidence to the commission and relates Ireland's historic grievances against British rule, going on to discuss the formation and
conduct of the Land League.

Life and Progress in Australasia (London, 1898) is much more
than a description of Davitt's visit to Australia and New Zealand in
1895. As a working journalist and public speaker he engaged with
the society he found and contrasted it with the Irish and British
systems at home. The book is a valuable source on Davitt's social
ideas.

The Boer Fight for Freedom (New York & London, 1902) is an
account of the Boer War from the Boer side. It contains fewer
descriptions of Davitt's own experiences than his book on
Australia.

*Within the Pale: The True Story of Anti-Semitic Persecutions in
Russia* (New York & London, 1903) is also a book about an issue.
Although much of it is based on dispatches he sent to the press
about the Kishinev pogrom, and he leaves us in no doubt about
his opinions on the matter, the autobiographical content is
limited.

Davitt's last and longest book, *The Fall of Feudalism in Ireland, or The Story of the Land League Revolution* (London, & New York, 1904), contains a good deal of Davitt's own story. It remains an important source on the history of the Land League.

Contemporary works that discuss Davitt include Wilfrid Scawen Blunt, *The Land War in Ireland: Being a Personal Narrative of Events* (London, 1912); William O'Brien, *Evening Memories* (Dublin & London, 1920) and *An Olive Branch in Ireland and its History* (London, 1910); Mrs William O'Brien *My Irish Friends* (Paris, 1937); H. M. Hyndman, *Further Reminiscences* (London, 1912); Laurence J. Kettle, (ed.), *The Material for Victory: The Memoirs of Andrew J. Kettle, Right-Hand Man to Charles S. Parnell* (Dublin, 1958); and an interesting account of the Ladies' Land League and critique of its work from inside the movement may be found in Anna Parnell, *The Tale of a Great Sham*, ed. Dana Hearne (Dublin, 1986).

There are two major biographies of Davitt. T. W. Moody, *Davitt and Irish Revolution, 1846–82* (Oxford, 1981) is by far the most thorough study and is an indispensable source for Davitt's life and times. Meticulously researched and detailed, the main content of the book ends with the 'Kilmainham Treaty', although a concluding chapter provides a summary of Davitt's life after 1882.

Francis Sheehy-Skeffington, *Michael Davitt: Revolutionary, Agitator and Labour Leader* (London, 1908; repr., London, 1967) treats the whole of Davitt's life and was written by a man who knew him and sympathised with his aims and ideas. Well-written and readable, it is limited by the fact that the author was denied access to Davitt's papers and the book was primarily based on published material.

A Russian historian, Valeria Emmanuilovna Kunina, published a study of Davitt's career, *Maikl Devitt, syn irlandskogo naroda: stranitsy zhizni i borby, 1846–1906* [*Michael Davitt, Son of the Irish People: Pages of Life and Struggle, 1846–1906*] (Moscow, 1973). It provides a general introduction to Davitt's life and to the land and political issues of the time, drawing on the works of Marx, Engels and Connolly on Ireland and sharing with Sheehy-Skeffington an interest in Davitt's role as a labour leader and editor of *Labour World*, in addition to treating his involvement in the land war.

Two other biographical works are D. B. Cashman, *The Life of Michael Davitt, Founder of the National Land League* (London, 1882), and M. M. O'Hara, *Chief and Tribune: Parnell and Davitt* (Dublin & London, 1919). These are both based on published sources and, while useful as far as they go, provide little in the way of historical analysis.

John Devoy produced a series of articles under the title 'Michael Davitt's Career', written just after Davitt's death and published in *Gaelic American* (New York), pts i–vii (9 June–3 Nov. 1906); repr. in *Irish Freedom*, 1913–14. These provide valuable, if partisan, accounts of Davitt's Fenian and Clan na Gael connections.

In addition to biographies of Davitt there are some useful shorter works which treat particular aspects of his career. John Dunleavy's pamphlet *Michael Davitt and Haslingden* (Haslingden, 1979) is a concise and well-researched account of the Davitt family when they lived in Haslingden. T. W. Moody, 'Michael Davitt' in J. W. Boyle (ed.), *Leaders and Workers* (Cork, 1965), pp 47–55, provides a brief overview of his career. Specific themes addressed by Professor Moody in articles include: 'Michael Davitt and the "Pen" Letter', *Irish Historical Studies*, iv, no. 15 (Mar. 1945), pp 224–53; 'Michael Davitt in Penal Servitude, 1870–77', *Studies*, xxx, no. 120 (Dec. 1941), pp 517–30; xxxi, no. 121 (Mar. 1942), pp 16–30; 'The New Departure in Irish Politics, 1878–9' in H. A. Cronne, T. W. Moody and D. B. Quinn (eds), *Essays in British and Irish History in honour of James Eadie Todd* (London, 1949), pp 303–33; 'Michael Davitt and the British Labour Movement, 1882–1906', *Transactions of the Royal Historical Society*, 5th ser., iii, (1953), pp 53–76.

Paul Bew, 'Parnell and Davitt' in D. George Boyce and Alan O'Day (eds), *Parnell in Perspective* (London, 1991), pp 38–51, provides a thought-provoking analysis and comparison of the two leaders. John Slatter, 'An Irishman at a Revolutionary Court of Honour: from the Michael Davitt Papers', *Irish Slavonic Studies*, no. 5 (1984), pp 33–42, provides a glimpse of a little-known side of Davitt, namely his contact with Polish and Russian revolutionaries. Carla King, 'Michael Davitt and the Kishinev Pogrom, 1903', *Irish Slavonic Studies*, no. 17 (1996), pp 19–43, examines Davitt's role as a foreign correspondent and investigator of the Kishinev pogrom in Bessarabia.

Important works that provide a broader context include: chapters by R. V. Comerford in W. E. Vaughan (ed.), *A New History of Ireland*, vi: *Ireland under the Union, II: 1870–1921* (Oxford, 1996); Pauric Travers, *Settlements and Divisions: Ireland 1870–1922* (Dublin, 1988).

On the land question, Paul Bew, *Land and the National Question in Ireland, 1858–82* (Dublin, 1978) and *Conflict and Conciliation in Ireland, 1890–1910: Parnellites and Radical Agrarians* (Oxford, 1987) are invaluable, as are Philip Bull, *Land, Politics and Nationalism: A Study of the Irish Land Question* (Dublin, 1996); Samuel Clark, *Social Origins of the Irish Land War* (Princeton, 1979); J. S. Donnelly, *The Land and the People of Nineteenth-Century Cork: The Rural Economy and the Land Question* (London & Boston, 1975); and on the Mayo background to the Land League, Donald Jordan, *Land and Popular Politics in Ireland: County Mayo from the Plantation to the Land War* (Cambridge, 1994).

On the political issues of the period see: D. George Boyce (ed.), *The Revolution in Ireland, 1879–1923* (Dublin, 1988); F. S. L. Lyons, *The Irish Parliamentary Party, 1890–1910* (London, 1951) and *The Fall of Parnell, 1890–91* (London, 1960); Conor Cruise O'Brien, *Parnell and His Party, 1880–90* (Oxford, 1957); Alan O'Day, *The English Face of Irish Nationalism: Parnellite Involvement in British Politics, 1880–86* (Dublin, 1977), *Parnell and the First Home Rule Episode, 1884–87* (Dublin 1986) and *Irish Home Rule, 1867–1921* (Manchester, 1998); Fintan Lane, *The Origins of Modern Irish Socialism* (Cork, 1997); Donal P. McCracken, *The Irish Pro-Boers, 1877–1902* (Johannesburg, 1988).

Biographies of Davitt's contemporaries include: F. S. L. Lyons, *John Dillon: A Biography* (London, 1968) and *Charles Stewart Parnell* (London, 1977); Paul Bew, *C. S. Parnell* (Dublin, 1980) and *John Redmond* (Dublin, 1996); Alan O'Day, *Charles Stewart Parnell* (Dublin, 1998); Frank Callanan, *T. M. Healy* (Cork, 1996); Sally Warwick-Haller, *William O'Brien and the Irish Land War* (Dublin, 1990).

HISTORICAL ASSOCIATION OF IRELAND

Life and Times Series

●

'The Historical Association of Ireland is to be congratulated for its **Life and Times** Series of biographies. They are written in an authoritative, accessible and enjoyable way'

History Ireland

'Invaluable *Life and Times* series'

Irish Times

'Students, tutors and the reading public will appreciate these short snapshots of key personalities'

Irish Historical Studies

'An excellent series'

John A. Murphy, Sunday Independent

●

No. 1 — HENRY GRATTAN
by JAMES KELLY

'The series has set a rigorous standard with this short study'

Books Ireland

'A succinct and thoughtful account of Grattan's career'

Eighteenth-Century Ireland

No. 2 — SIR EDWARD CARSON
by ALVIN JACKSON

'A scintillating essay in reappraisal'

K. Theodore Hoppen, Irish Historical Studies

'Jackson's splendid *Sir Edward Carson*'

Irish Times

No. 3 — EAMON DE VALERA
by PAURIC TRAVERS

'A good short summary of a very long political life'

Stair

No. 4 — D. P. MORAN
by PATRICK MAUME

'Written with a fine sense of detachment and objectivity'

Leader

No. 5 — HANNA SHEEHY SKEFFINGTON
by MARIA LUDDY

'Recommended without reservation'

Books Ireland

No. 6 — SHANE O'NEILL
by CIARAN BRADY

'A richly documented analysis'

John A. Murphy, Sunday Independent

'An exciting book. A little masterpiece'

Denis Faul, Seanchas Ard Mhacha

No. 7 — JUSTIN McCARTHY
by EUGENE J. DOYLE

'Successfully confutes F. S. L. Lyons's picture of McCarthy
as a weak and vacillating successor to Parnell'

Irish Historical Studies

No. 8 — JOHN REDMOND
by PAUL BEW

'Bew brings an assured touch to the nuances of the historical
context and of Redmond's political attitudes and strategy'

John A. Murphy, Sunday Independent

'A brief stimulating assessment of Redmond's political career'

Irish Historical Studies